Boys Adrift: a response to a seminal book

by Kenneth Hawkins

ISBN-13: 978-1492976363
ISBN-10: 1492976369

Table of Contents

Dedication

This book is dedicated to my family, including my most excellent wife, wonderful daughters, brother, sister, and parents. It is dedicated also to my wife's family, from whom I have learned so much, and who so graciously tolerated my many errors. It is dedicated to all of those who helped me, especially when they had no reason to do so. It is dedicated to all those teachers who put their hearts into their work, and dealt with the bureaucratic foolishness to somehow do their jobs.

Sensei means "born before", in Japanese. It is used to describe spiritual and martial arts masters. The idea is that they are farther down the path, and thus can help the seeker.

I dedicate this book to the Sensei who helped me, and to those who will benefit from this book.

I have a five year old daughter. I wrote this book, in part, to improve the environment for the guy she will marry. I love you so very much, little girl, and I am doing all I can for you, unto the seventh generation.

Introduction

I was originally going to write an email to Dr. Sax, saying what is in this book. However, it got too big, so I'm going another route. The text was written over a period of three days. For some reason, this just flowed through my fingers into the computer.

Wisdom is refined from experience, and reading, and thinking about things. Good judgment is part of wisdom. Good judgment comes from refining simple rules about life, which comes from experience, which is generated by making choices, often from poor judgment. Life is about making choices.

Will Rogers, the comedian of the 1920's and 30's, made the observation that there are three ways to learn.

The first way is by <u>reading</u>. But few people do this. Those in college tend to do this, though.

The second way is to learn by <u>watching the mistakes of others</u>[1]. But few do this.

The vast majority of people choose to learn by urinating on the electric fence for themselves. Or as Benjamin Franklin put it, the school of hard experience charges a high tuition, but most people refuse to learn elsewhere.

This book is for people in the first and second class. Those in the third class will find that pain is an infinitely patient teacher, who continues her teaching until the lesson is completely learned, and sometimes longer.

Boys Adrift is a fascinating book. As with all books, it left out some points. Let me begin by saying that I agree with everything Dr. Sax says in his book. He is right on target, as far as he goes. No book can cover everything, however, and I had hoped to fill in some of the gaps.

---

1 Pain is a very useful teacher. The best way to experience it is in someone else's body, as they screw up.

I graduated from college with a 3.5, majoring in Anthropology, and a Near Eastern language. I worked more than full time, while going to college full time. I paid about 2/3 of my college costs myself, by working. I have a M.A. Degree in Near Eastern Studies, for which I had to demonstrate proficiency in three languages: two Near Eastern languages, and a European language. My M.A. Thesis was a partial translation of a history of the Persian-speaking parts of the Middle East. The thesis is over 300 pages long.

I work for a bank now. My annual earnings are in the low six figures, however I live below my means, and bank it. I am married, and have two children. My bright, talented older daughter is married, to a fantastic guy, no less so because he is a younger version of me, with the same kind of interests. My younger daughter is already a comedian, making people laugh.

Chapter 1: Response to The Riddle

A. Examine the incentive structure

My wife once tutored a boy just like what Dr. Sax describes, in Spain. The kid was extremely bright, with horrible grades. He could hear something once, and retain it. He didn't want to retain it, however. So he would sing songs, in his head, to block out the information.

He was an only child, and his parents were very worried about him. At the time, I was sending my soon-to-be-wife *Star Wars* toys, and books, which she would give him as a reward for studying. He had driven his other tutors crazy. He loved the Star Wars movies, however, and would work for Star Wars toys and books.

They got his emotions going[2]. That is very important. The comedian Jerry Seinfeld has a routine where he notes that comic book superheroes are not fantasy figures, they are options, for the guys reading the comic book. People live their stories. The stories boys get in school usually do not excite them, and do not arouse their emotions, so they go elsewhere.

I told my wife to tell him that if he mastered English, there were schools that taught Jedi skills in the U.S. He became very interested in mastering English. I understood incentives.

After I read Tom Brown, Jr's first book, *The Tracker*, I knew I had to go to his school. I liked it so much that I worked with my sister to get my nephew there, as well. He learned a lot.

Tom Brown, Jr., as a boy, asked his teacher how to understand owls. His teacher said, "Go ask the mice". Brown puzzled this over, and finally realized that the behavior of owls reflects the behavior of mice. Animal behavior is easy to figure out: they go to where the food is. That is their incentive. Boys go where the emotional rush is, if they are getting enough food.

When you understand incentives, you understand human behavior.

---

2 If you can find a way to lead a boy into an emotional rush, of excitement, fascination, and so on, through learning, you have your incentive.

Early in the history of Xerox, Joe Wilson couldn't figure out why the newer, better machine wasn't selling, compared to the older, crummier machine. Then he figured out that the salespeople got a larger commission with the older machine.

My father told me about how the highways in West Virginia were constructed, prior to the 1960's. They paid the contractors by the mile, not by the highway section completed. So the highways have many hairpin turns, and their length is more than double the distance they could have been.

My father oversaw a contractor, doing core drilling. They were paid by the day. They had an ancient rig, that frequently broke down. On a good day, they drilled 50 feet. The contract was changed, to pay by the foot. The rig was pulled out, that day, and an efficient new rig installed, which never failed to get less than 200 feet per day.

Years ago, I worked for a security guard company, in college. We had a guard who found and put out a just set fire, on a bulletin board, in a wooden building of the college. He was a hero. He was praised to the entire staff of guards. I was jealous; I'd done the job a long time, and never been able to do that. Then he found another fire, just as it was set, and put it out. The bosses were happy that he did this, but somehow not as enthusiastic. I was jealous. Two fires? I hadn't even found one.

Check this out. He found a THIRD fire, just as it was set! The bosses decided that anybody with that kind of luck needed to be in a better job, and they helped him make a career readjustment in that direction. Pigs get fat, hogs get slaughtered. Or, systemic pushback exists.

The Australian government once needed to reduce the dingo population. So they decided to pay the aborigines for dingo skins. The aborigines are smart people. They got paid for skins. How does one produce skins? With dingoes. How does one get dingoes? Hunting. How does one maximize income? Not with hunting. So they set up breeding populations. The dingo population tripled, before the government caught on.

Billy, cited on page 1 of Dr. Sax's book, loves to read. So do I. Billy memorized poems in Elvish. I have memorized Hawaiian Hula chants. Why doesn't Billy want to study? The reason is simple enough.

In the 9th grade, I spent an entire <u>year</u> of English class, going over what has to be the dreariest book I've ever read, *Silas Marner*. I read it through in less than two weeks. Then we crawled through the book.

I guess girls like books like that, or *Wuthering Heights*, but that book was torture for me. I was a very good student, who loved reading. Can you imagine how much worse the torture was for boys who weren't good students? It was like an inoculation- a small unpleasant dose, to keep you safe from the real thing, given every day of class.

I could race through Edgar Rice Burroughs' John Carter of Mars series of books, though. They were great. The movie just didn't do them justice. I love Sci Fi. I used to check out ten Sci Fi books at a time, from the library, and read them in a weekend.

Boys are indeed disengaging from school. What is the incentive to engage? It is too vague. Boys with parents who are well off, in particular, know they can slough off. I knew I had to do well in school, or my life would mean nothing. My parents told stories about the Great Depression, and WW II. I had motivation. I had one chance, in college, because my parents weren't about to support me, if I didn't make it. I had trouble, in my first year of college, until I learned how to study. Then I just got better, and better.

That is one reason immigrants tend to do well. They know they don't have anything to go back to. Dr. Sax notes this. Dr. Sax notes that boys aren't interested in much real world activity. Well, yes. What are the incentives[3]?

---

3 When my older daughter was in the 9th grade, I told her that her A's in Math and Science were worth $20, now, instead of just $5. She gave me a half hour lecture on how math was difficult for girls, she didn't have a head for math, and on and on. I sat and listened, patiently. When she ran out of steam, I said, "OK, honey, your first A in math is worth $200 to you, in cold, hard cash. That is 2 $100 bills, or 4 $50 bills, that will be placed in your hands, the day I see that first A in math. And I can say that with total assurance that I will never have to pay out, because you just told me there's no way you can do it." I said nothing more. 2 years later, after months of study with a boyfriend, she made that A. She didn't think I'd honor it. I said, "Oh no, I can't do it today, but you will have it all, tomorrow, every penny of it. If I make a promise, I keep it." I got off dirt cheap, it must have been something like 50c/hour. Price tutors, and you'll see what I mean. But

I am amazed to see elementary schools that have no recess. Girls may be able to sit. Boys can't. If I had not had recess, in grade school, it would have felt as if I was wrapped in plastic wrap. On P. 8 of Dr. Sax's book, one kid compared school to prison. This is one reason why.

B. Teachers aren't the only teachers

My sister raised a boy. She was smart. She got him into Tai Chi classes, at the age of 11. He also took Aikido. She pointed out, indirectly, that martial arts masters tended to be very aware, and alert, knowing far more than just what they teach in school. He got the hint, and did a lot of extra work. His instructor had him teaching the beginning students, at 16.

My sister and I got him to Tom Brown's school. I taught him a shamanic method to be invisible[4]. He could walk right by the assistant principal, and not be seen. But he got an emotional rush from doing well in school. I shared with him some ideas from the book *Photoreading, the whole mind system*. He would flip through his Spanish book, before a test, and outscore his girlfriend, who had studied for 2-3 hours the night before.

He was offered a four year scholarship, all expenses paid, at the state college, due to his academics. They liked him so much, they also made an offer to him, for free tuition, and a $17,000/year stipend, to get his Master's Degree, as well. They paid him to get his Master's. Would you say that a little guidance from older folks might have been helpful to him? Why don't we have more of that? There is a reason.

I had the advantage of Boy Scouts, as a kid. I talked to a guy in church who loved being a Boy Scout, as a kid. I asked why he wasn't a Scoutmaster. He said that one accusation of abuse would destroy his ability to take care of his family[5].

---

she did it all herself, far more cheaply, because I understood incentives. Study hard, get good job? Huh uh. Not real. Too abstract. What did she want? Mall fuel. Folding green. That worked. And with that under her belt, she went on to handle far more difficult issues, all by herself. I've never seen this in a book. I use what works. Properly designed incentives work.

4 The second Crocodile Dundee movie portrays this method in action.

5 Dr. Sax, at P. 170, cites Peggy Drexler, saying that women who don't have men in their personal lives can actively recruit men from family and community, to be in their son's lives. P. 92, *Raising Boys without Men: How maverick moms are creating the next generation of exceptional men,*

He wasn't willing to risk being able to take care of his family, to deal with emotionally unstable teenagers who know they can make false accusations, and won't ever be held to account for it. Pay careful attention to that. People react to disincentives, also. That is a pattern worth being very aware of.

The book *Blossoming the Child,* by Tamarack Song, addresses how to raise boys, in a healthy way, based on what works in indigenous cultures. The author has a section in that book on how ADD is actually a plus. Native Americans identified these kids at the age of five or so, and had special training for them.

Native people taught by direct experience. Let's consider learning about plants. The white man culture way is to start with the name, maybe a picture. They discuss it, in a boring way, and then there's a test. The boy may not even get to see the real plant. The theory is rarely grounded in practice.

The native way is to have the kid look at, touch, smell, maybe even taste the real plant, first. The boy learns the complete life cycle of the plant, what its favored conditions are- sun, shade, acidic or basic soil, preferred companions, and so on. At the very end of the lesson, after the awareness of it is thoroughly grounded, the boy learns the name of the plant.

No test is necessary, because the knowledge, the direct awareness, was burnt in. It would be like taking a test on one's knowledge of a friend.

C. The Apathy Virus: What is the context?

I cannot disagree with anything Dr. Sax has to say, here. I would say, however, that he does not appear to be considering the diet of the boys. My sister made sure her son ate a very good diet. This means no junk food, few to no refined carbs, no soda, minimal to no sugar.

Emmaus, PA: Rodale, 2006. Dr. Sax, I believe you forgot that society likes to crucify responsible men. It's so easy to refer people. I walk the path, myself, first, before I direct other people down it. I spoke with a woman, whose family had taken in a teenaged girl, who had nowhere to go. She started talking about molestation, which had not occurred. The family invited her to leave, immediately, as there is no defense against such an accusation.

She didn't deny him junk food, she just pointed out that it makes people feel bad[6]. He chose, of his own volition, to avoid it. The diet she had him on was alkalinizing. I am not a doctor, so I could not offer any medical advice, of course, and this is, accordingly, no kind of medical advice.

However, I have observed that every indigenous culture I've ever looked at started their healing by cleaning out the intestines, and then going on an alkalinizing diet. George Ohsawa and Dr. D.C. Jarvis pointed out decades ago that none of the disease germs can survive in a body with alkaline pH.

Dr. Jarvis points out that an alkaline body sucks the moisture out of harmful bacteria, and they die. He noted that the traditional Vermont cure for alcoholism is to alkalinize. He recommends, as an example, a tablespoon of old-fashioned apple cider vinegar[7], like the Bragg stuff today; with a tablespoon of raw honey, in water- all are alkalinizing-drunk once an hour, till the addiction passes, as it does when the body hits a pH of about 7.1.

Fresh lemon juice can substitute for the vinegar. Lemonade was at one time an alkalinizing health drink.

The Apathy Virus, as Dr. Sax calls it, is totally consistent with what I've seen among people with acidic body pH. This is not easy to measure, directly. Saliva and blood pH are not body pH. The standard American diet is nutritionally barren- which means hunger, which means people eat much more, and get fat. It is also more acidifying than any diet I've ever looked at. We will discuss this later, in more detail.

Not caring about school, or much of anything beyond video games and TV, is something I've seen often. I have yet to see people with these issues, who were not also eating an acidifying diet with a toxic load.

I got some of my ideas on diet, including how to detox, from Dr. Richard Schulze. His book *Common Sense Health and Healing* is a free download, at his website, herbdoc.com.

---

6 It's low in nutrition, and high in toxic load. This is not a useful combination.
7 Sugar is not acidic, but it causes acidic conditions. Old-fashioned vinegar is not the same as the rotgut sold in grocery stores today.

Dr. Batmanghelidj's books discuss dehydration in Americans, which is also acidifying. Paul Bragg's books discuss fresh, raw foods in diet. I'm sure there are other good books in the area. I haven't yet found a good book on alkalinizing diet. I've had to put my ideas together from different sources.

Dr. John Christopher was at a vitamin conference, for some reason. They asked him to speak. He said he had seen a lot of nice displays, and so on, but he had one question to ask them- "HOW CAN WHAT IS DEAD GIVE YOU LIFE?" He was invited to leave, immediately.

I'll ask that question- how can food that comes in its own convenient coffin give you life? Junk food is dead food. Look at what criminals eat. I guarantee you it is acidifying[8]. My grandparents, and parents, always had a garden, and ate fresh food from it. Their eggs were fresh, and hadn't been sitting in a warehouse for a month or two. They rarely went to restaurants, and when they did, the food hadn't been sitting in a freezer since it was made up, six months prior.

Diet is destiny. Diet is life, and life energy level, even income.

The media discusses diet. I told a friend of mine some of the above. He found an article in the newspaper- not an advertisement, an article, actually quoting a nutritionist, that said Ding-Dongs are good for you. The first question I asked him was who paid for the article? Cui bono? I then asked him what was in Ding Dongs. I then said, "If these are so good for you, eat a dozen, and see how you feel."

Do that, with the junk food today. If I eat junk food in quantity, I feel like I've taken drugs. I am jumpy, and easily irritable. Junk food gives me the behavior of a junkie. An addict. In a single day. What is it like for a boy fed this stuff regularly, for a long time, I wonder?

---

8 One of the Police Academy movies had a criminal character complaining about all the junk food, and lack of vegetarian fare, in a store. I almost fell off my chair, laughing.

What have you noticed, about how diet affects your behavior?

What foods or supplements are you taking, to give you energy? To make you feel better? How effective are they?

What kind of diet are you eating, when you are apathetic?

What kind of toxic load are you carrying in your body? Have you tried a serious detoxification?

If you have children, have you noticed how they imitate you? In noticing that, what desire do you also notice, to ensure that they have a good example, in you, to imitate?

Chapter 2: Changes at school that discriminate against boys

Dr. Sax is right on target, here. Let's fire for effect. Our culture seems to think that we need to deconstruct gender roles, and make boys androgynous. Do we have any examples in history, where this was sustainable? There were some examples of this in Rome, later on. The barbarians rolled them over, but they were dying out anyway. There are also numerous examples of fanatical ideologies being applied, all throughout history, which were as functional as the Emperor's New Clothes.

A. Polarity

I studied Yin and Yang polarity for a long time, out of fascination. There isn't much awareness of polarity in the USA. In Spanish, French, German, Thai, and Arabic, that I know of, there is far more gender, in language, and culture. These people are more aware of polarity.

What is polarity? Polarity is an energy gradient. If you have a distinct difference in voltage, between two poles, and a circuit, you get current. I used to short out batteries, when I was a kid, with a wire. The battery is then useless. It has no "juice", or energy gradient, or charge, or life.

For humans, that current is life. The French say *Vive le difference* for a reason. *Le difference est la vie.* The difference is life. If you do more of what makes you feel good, in the long run[9], you feel good, and you have more life[10].

Yin is usually considered the female polarity, and Yang the male molarity. However nobody is a pure type, there is always a mix of the two. Even the Yin Yang symbol has a little Yang, in the Yin, and a little Yin, in the Yang.

Latin and Oriental women, and even Russian women, understand polarity. When they are comfortably in their Yin polarity, I can feel it crackling from a distance.

---

9   Notice that tag line, as it is very, very important.
10   Orgasm is the discharge of built up life force energy, or Chi, the depletion of an energy gradient. It is possible to retain that Chi in the body, during orgasm, with Chi Kung or Yogic methods. However that is well beyond the scope of this book.

The book *French or Foe* notes that French women 80 years old will dress up, before going out, in case they meet somebody[11]. Many do. Why? Latin, and particularly French, women are comfortable in their bodies. Paris is incredible, in part, due to this. Anglo women usually aren't, and many seem to want to ensure that others aren't, also.

I know a Puerto Rican woman, who had to leave her husband, many years ago, because he was a drunk. She raised her three children by herself. One was a son. She understood polarity, however. She got him into Boy Scouts, and made sure he was otherwise around real, responsible men. She knew and accepted that she couldn't do it for him. He was an Army Ranger[12], and is now in corporate America, in an executive job. Her daughters married well, and have great jobs.

What would many an Anglo women have done? She would have railed against men, kept the son away from real men, and her son would have had a major gap in his education. But Anglo women often don't care about men, even their own sons[13].

I know this will sound odd, in today's culture. Women simply don't know what it is to be a man, any more than a man knows what it is to be a woman. They might have a mental model, but they don't know. Latin, Oriental, African, and Polynesians understand this, and also polarity, but Anglo culture prefers to live in denial.

R.M. Johnson, in his book *Why Men Fear Marriage,* notes that boys need advice from someone who has been down the path they are on[14]. The hormonal flows in teenage boys [and girls] make them crazy, by any adult measure.

Traditionally, in most cultures, the old teach the young. In our culture, we have a better idea: we warehouse old people, and let them rot. Is it any wonder we have 14 year old parents? They have no guidance.

---

11 I saw this myself, in France, however if someone else also documented it, you know it is more than just my observation.

12 Ranger school is a major ordeal. You might sleep an hour at night. They do a lot of dangerous stuff. The men love it.

13 I know someone who works with psychiatric patients. One of them was the son of a single mother. The mother would sunbathe nude, in full view of her teen son, regularly. How stupid is that? Mothers in any other culture know better. Nudism is something different.

14 I could say that any fool in my father's generation knew this, but we have forgotten the simple truths of life. I cite the book, so you know I'm not the only one saying this.

I remember reading that women overseas don't like American culture, because they don't want their daughters to turn out like Britney Spears. I didn't want it, either, for my daughter. I wonder what kind of relationship advice Brit is getting. Her history of marriages seems somewhat checkered, which suggests that it's not very good.

Dr. Sax notes that boys' brains develop differently. So they do. American education spends more money per pupil than most other developed countries, and accomplishes less. This is unfortunately typical[15].

Working with kids is too much work, for people with an acidic body chemistry, so let them watch TV, and play video games, and take drugs. Leo Buscaglia noted 20 years ago that the average American child entering the first grade had seen over 6,000 graphically portrayed murders, on TV, not counting other violence[16]. That was before the violent video games Dr. Sax refers to.

Dr. Sax talks about the difference between *Wissenshaft*, or book learning, and *Kenntniss*, or actual experience, at p. 28. Actual experience is sadly missing in schools. Let's talk about one way this could start happening. I know a guy who used to do storytelling in schools, as a volunteer.

He would bring along an Osage Orange bow, that he made himself, stone or steel tomahawks, baskets, berry mashers, an Atlatl, other tools, buckskin clothing, and so on. He said the boys were intently alert, for these presentations. He told stories in the old-fashioned way, that is, describing scenes from a screen of the mind, shortening or lengthening the story depending on the attention span of the audience.

---

15 Americans also spend more money on medicine, per capita, than any other country, to get results that are 73rd among nations. 72 countries get more bang for their medical buck than ours. The main reason for this is lobbyists. Congress makes laws that are best for corporations, not for people. Another reason is that Americans love denial. They also like to defer, or deflect, responsibility.

16 Let's use a comparison, to put that in perspective. The average American child of 20 years ago had seen more murders, on TV, at 6 years of age, than some SS concentration camp guards, during WW II. Is anybody doing anything to reduce this visual diet of murder? No, and if anything portrayals of murders are getting more numerous, and graphic, in the media.

One story he enjoyed telling was *The Genie and the Hair*[17]. He told stories with great feeling. For The Three Little Pigs, he had the kids act out being the wolf, the pigs, and the houses. Once, he ran out of stories, and reached to a shelf, to get a book to read. One of the boys said, "No, tell us one of your stories, they're better!"

The girls were interested, he said. But the boys were transfixed, they paid total and complete attention, there was never a problem getting them to listen. He told stories with the emotional rush of being in the story. I notice that wilderness skills school students are about 90% male. The learning is all actual experience.

How does the media help? They've decided the Boy Crisis is a myth. One thing I've learned is that most of what I see and hear in the news media is a lie[18]. There was a time when reporters were respected, in this country. They did real service. It is no accident that Superman's alter ego is a reporter.

But the quality of reporting has tanked, badly. I don't expect the media will do much of anything useful. So it is no accident that the balance to the article on the Myth of the Boy Crisis, of p. 40, of Dr. Sax's book, never went anywhere. Reich Minister of Propaganda Josef Goebbels propaganda was more balanced than the foolishness we see in our media.

Lord of the Flies. What a stupid book. *How would you feel if you were piggy?* Huh? I had no interest in answering that question, in school. I already felt that way. I wanted to feel like an aggressor, to know I could at least do damage to those tormenting me, and maybe even stare them in the eye, and let the animal inside out, and have them back down in fear. I wanted to be able to look at them, and see them cringe. That was my polarity, at the time.

Competition. It has its place. I think, now, that cooperation is far more interesting, because you get better results[19]. However, cooperation in a context of competition is basically what sports are.

---

17 I found it on Amazon, under that title, as a kid's book.
18 I remember a teacher telling me that the only machine more efficient at telling lies than a printing press was a videocamera.
19 Riane Eisler speaks of cooperative cultures. They worked better than ours.

Remember the guy who used to bring Native American tools into school classes? A boy once admonished him about bringing a bow, without an arrow, because you can't bring weapons to school. Oh, that's comforting, apparently the violence in schools I've read about is another media myth. I feel so much better. You can't bring weapons to school.

Of course students can bring weapons into schools; there are simply consequences. In my father's high school, students would bring new firearms to school, for show and tell. The teachers had no objections, as there were no problems. What changed, since then? TV and visual diet, the diet of food, and societal attitudes.

Boys Adrift discussed the kid who wrote a story about a German prison camp during WW II, and was referred for psychiatric evaluation. How stupid is that? Zero tolerance for violence? Lately American educational policy seems like a black hole of stupidity. We have only to look at its results, with boys. We can argue all we want, but results are the only report card. How well is American education serving boys? Let's quote them- "It sucks" "It's boring".

I served in the U.S. Army. Yes, I learned about weapons. Did I misuse them? No. I heard a story, probably apocryphal, about a Marine reservist being interviewed by a female reporter. He mentioned teaching firearm safety to teenage boys[20].

The reporter was shocked, and asked him why he was teaching them to be killers. He said he wasn't. She said he was teaching them the equipment. He asked her why she was teaching people to be a prostitute. She was offended, and denied this. He said, "Well, you have the equipment for it."

Here is a thought: one really needs to be mature, to have weapons. Except in the U.S. media. I don't like violence in the media. Is it Steven Segal who won't do a film unless at least 200 people get killed, on screen? Or Bruce Willis? Does it matter?

---

20 In the South, and West, this is a rite of passage, even more so than the driver's license. The first introduction to firearms means you are no longer a boy, you are a man, and you need to learn how to act like a man. If you read war stories, you find stories such as *Band of Brothers*, where a redneck who grew up with his rifle saved his buddies, time and time again. Alvin York, and Audie Murphy, were like this.

Hollywood seems to want to promote grossly disrespectful behavior, including violence. I'd rather see movies that make me think.

Violence is, regrettably, part of life. It shows up in the books of Hemingway, Steinbeck, Dostoyevsky, all the ancient Greek myths, Tolstoy, Shakespeare, and many others. So, the zero tolerance for violence is going to get rid of 95% of Western literature, is that it? This is what education has come to?

Schools have gotten bigger, and students more anonymous. This is unfortunate. One room schoolhouses turned out a great product, because students helped each other. But we have to have the tyranny of the grade level, instead.

B. There is a better way to deal with violence

My uncle used to punch his horses. They would jump. Then he'd give them their shots, and they wouldn't jump. He prepared them, with a small dose up front. We need something to defuse useless violence. It exists.

I believe the martial arts should be taught to every boy and girl in school, who wants to learn them. Why? Because these arts channel all the physical energy both get. They teach them respect. They teach them to stand their ground. They make bullying more difficult, and less likely to happen. Most importantly, they teach finesse. A beginning martial artist practices many blows. The advanced student can end a conflict with one blow, using intuition.

The master never needs to strike a blow, because s/he anticipated the problem, and sidestepped it. Never needing to strike a blow- that is zero violence, not zero tolerance for violence, isn't it? If you have zero tolerance for something, that means you are reacting to it, which means it is still going on. It's probably also repressed, which means it blows up without warning.

The martial arts teach discipline, making quick choices, and that choices and actions have consequences. They teach the value of sustained effort, over time, with incremental reviews and benchmarking.

I personally prefer the Chinese spiritual martial arts, however all of them have their place. Tai Chi at the beginning of the school day would set a great tone, especially for boys.

Dividing students into Blue and White phratries is a great idea, thanks for putting this in your book, Dr. Sax. Having a Hogwarts style collection of points to the group is a fantastic metaphor for giving to the group, to the larger self. This is a skill that separates real, mature adults from children.

Being the kid who gets the wrong answer, who costs the whole team, is a very good lesson to learn for life- young- when the cost for doing so is very small. It doesn't work for girls, so well. But then, that's not what this book is about.

C. Self Esteem

Confidence is competence, for boys. If they can do anything well, they feel confident. School needs to set boys up for success, not failure. Team competition means learning to work with different kinds of people. It is as important for boys as self-esteem seems to be for girls. Right on, Dr. Sax!

Girls need to be built up. Boys have to be broken down- towards a real, tangible goal. I saw this right and left in the military. Read Richard Marcinko's novels, or any of the books by SEALS, to get some idea how Navy SEALS talk to each other, if you doubt this.

Let me say that again. Confidence is competence. The kid who played video football went out to play the real thing, and gained confidence, due to having mastered something physical. That kind of confidence floods throughout their entire system. Overcoming serious obstacles entrains the entire system in success.

My sister knew she had to keep her son fascinated. She got him into Tai Chi and Aikido classes. She told him to learn woodcarving at the Senior Center, which he did. For boys, confidence is competence. If a boy can do something good, something worthy of admiration, he feels competent. School doesn't set boys up for that, much, any more. Maybe that's one reason why boys experience school as lockdown.

How do we set up boys, to help them become competent, young?

How can we keep boys busy, in those activities that give them confidence, so they learn more, and better?

How do we introduce boys to the spiritual side of life, since all deep satisfaction in life comes from that side?

How do we train boys to become responsible adults, early?

Chapter 3: Video games are addictive

I love video games. Eight hours would go by in a flash. I had to make the decision to cut them off, cold turkey. They were too addictive. The chemicals generated in the brain had an addicting effect, for me. And that was as an adult. I wasn't about to waste quarters in video machines, when I was younger, that could be spent on books.

I was a nerd in high school. I read as much Sci Fi as I could. Why? Because it was interesting. There was action. There was Tan Hadron, and Sanoma Tora, and Tavia. And many others. You don't know who those people are, probably, but I did. Tan Hadron- now there was a guardian warrior. I saw Sanoma Toras in school, and even married one, and had to leave her, for the same reasons Tan Hadron had to.

My father bought a lot of books. He would let me read them, because I'd finish them in a night. Books were my escape, from the nasty, brutish, cruel reality of secondary education. For my brother, it was alcohol. For my sister, it was playing with animals.

Video games are an escape, from a dreary existence. It wasn't always this way. I had a friend, who went camping in a New England winter, in January, with the Boy Scouts. That wouldn't happen now, they are too worried about liability. I look at the way the Boy Scout Handbook has been dumbed down, even since I was a kid, and, well, no wonder boys are bored. It was meaningful enough for him that he remembered every detail, 40 years later.

The one thing I will always remember, of high school, was the cheerleaders, the eye candy. Who did they go with? Football players. They were generally very physical, and not very bright. Some were abusive. What is the lesson, for the boys? Be big, not very bright, and abusive, to get the eye candy. Is that really the lesson we want to teach boys?

I am big, well I could have played football, but reading did a lot more for me. I notice that those cheerleaders seem to have become more intelligent, over time; those I could follow up on seem to have found brighter guys, and left the jocks long ago.

But high school students don't know that. I was picked on, a lot, in high school, until I took Karate classes. I also learned to cut people apart, with my tongue. I was vicious. People learned to leave me alone. There is an 8 year old boy near where I live, now, who told my wife he had to be a different person, a much harsher person, in school.

Video games are an escape. Are boys addicted to video games any different from sports addicts, who waste an entire day in front of the TV? No, they are just copying what they see. Children don't listen, they imitate their parents.

I do so love computers. However, I also spend time outdoors, and at the beach. Too much time on a computer leads precisely to the cultural autism described at p. 30 of Dr. Sax's book. I remember drill sergeants in the Army, dealing with TV addicts. What did they do? They spoke loudly, and involved them in extensive physical exercise, until they were broken of it.

Boys don't get many chances to do well, in school. Artificial worlds where one can succeed are very attractive. Is this so unusual? 40% of all books in print are Romance novels. I know guys don't read them, so who does that leave? Are make believe worlds really so foreign, even to women? I have read Romance novels, as part of my education, with some difficulty, but I forced myself through a couple. Some are quite pornographic, a sort of wish fulfillment. So, fantasy wish fulfillment is ok for women, but not for men, is that it?

"Romance novels for guys", as one female bookstore clerk I knew called them, or adventure novels, are very popular, also. Dr. Sax, you note that boys get mature about the age of 30 or so. Yes, that's right, in my experience. Prior to that time, they need input, what some would call role models, and opportunities to expand their skills, and develop themselves.

Let's look back 200 years. A man had to have channels of income, to support a family. Generally by the age of 30, he was known, and parents could trust their daughters to him. Given shorter life spans, women got married younger, so they had more time for bearing children. 200 years ago, the infant mortality rate was unbelievably high.

Boys most particularly need to learn patience. I learned this by studying music, and the martial arts. Going fishing, years ago, also taught this. Tom Brown, Jr., was set by his Apache teacher to study animal tracks, in a meditative state, for up to 12 hours. They would actually watch the track degrade, in the weather. They loved every minute of it. Teenage boys, 12 hours, totally entranced as they learned. Ummm, why isn't this used in schools?

Dr. Sax, what you said about boys today preferring video games to being with girls is right on. I've seen that myself.

At p. 92, Dr. Sax notes that crack cocaine affects the same part of the brain that video games do. This is no surprise to me.

Video games are addictive. I choose not to play them. I also choose not to drink alcohol, or take any illegal drugs. I stay away even from legal drugs. I don't watch TV in English any more. I have better ways to enjoy myself.

Dr. Sax, you're right, that's the attitude we need to foster. I am so glad you wrote your book, to spread this.

What needs are video games satisfying, that aren't being met in the world of shared consensus reality?

How could those needs be met, in a healthier way, in the world of shared consensus reality?

Chapter 4: ADHD Medications

I think the idea of delaying kindergarten, a year, for boys, makes a lot of sense. Yet I myself did first and second grade, in one year. I could have graduated high school in three years, and gone to college at 16. I chose to stay in high school another year.

My cousin had two boys, in Junior High. The teachers wanted to give them speed. Whatever happened to "just say no to drugs"? He said "No, thank you", and pulled them out of school, to be home-schooled. He got textbooks, and they did their work, at home.

He put them in community college classes, while still in High School, and when they graduated high school, they both had 2 years of college courses. They are both bright, polite, and very good at what they do. The only thing I would note is that they are somewhat sheltered. One of them, the one who speaks five languages, decided to go into the Army, without telling his parents. On his own, he sought out an ordeal, as part of his education. I and his parents would have tried to talk him out of it, but he didn't ask us.

I had all the signs of ADHD when I was a kid. My mother was a teacher. She simply kept me busy. I always had books to read, from the age of 3, on. She made sure I went to Boy Scouts, and any other activity like that. Her attitude was, if you had trouble in school, that meant you worked harder and longer. So I did.

My mother remembers a time when the "chair" of education stood on four legs: community, church, home, and school. *The War on Parents*, by Cornell Lewis, notes that community has largely eroded. Church is eroding. Home[21]? It's nowhere near what it used to be. So now, one teacher is going to make up for the collapse of the other three legs of the chair?

---

21 I was in school, in the South, when public schools were forcibly desegregated by Federal court order. They also moved teachers around. My school picked up a black teacher, whose teaching method was to read out loud, from the book. Now that sounds old-fashioned. Why did he do that? Well, in the schools he went to, and taught in, there weren't enough textbooks for the students. Any time a student misbehaved, he would ask them, "Where yo' home trainin' is, boy?" He was using shame. He was saying that their behavior reflected on their family. Orientals use this to great effect. What does it say, that Americans have no shame at all, now? There are better teaching methods, yes- positive reinforcement- but shame can't be used any more.

Dr. Richard Schulze has noted that ADHD kids existed thirty years ago, but they weren't harassing teachers with having to teach too many kids, teach to the test, deal with extremely unrealistic standards, and a lack of support from the educational hierarchy. They also had community, church, and home, to back up education, then. The drugs are an easy out.

Many Americans in positions of authority seem little better than fools. School shooters were apparently almost all on legal drugs. Has anybody done anything to fix the brutality in school, the violence in the media, and drugs, that created them to be shooters? Of course not. Americans seem to have lost the ability to see what causes problems, or to have any will to fix them. They are good at stepping on each other's rights, and fighting about it.

I understand some research has been done in relating diet to ADHD behavior. I'm not surprised. When I eat junk food, I go into recognizable ADHD behavior myself. I am very sensitive to junk food. I can't even eat in most fast food restaurants.

Drugs have no side effects. Drugs have effects. I am fascinated to hear advertisements for drugs, for depression, on TV, where they cite side effects such as thoughts of suicide. OK, so you have someone who is depressed. You're going to give them a drug, that makes them think about suicide? What did I miss here? What's wrong with this picture?

I know a woman who used to be an agent for a pharmaceutical company. She was orally admonished if she didn't spend at least $10,000/week on premium items to give to doctors-as incentives to prescribe her company's drugs- twenty years ago[22]. You won't see stuff like that in the media, because they don't care. You won't hear this from any authority figure. All I ask, is that you think about the incentives here.

What is the incentive for the media? To sell you products. They are not in the business of educating you, or building you up, or helping you, or doing anything for you. They are solely and only in the business of selling you products you mostly don't need.

---

22 Interestingly enough, she was also a cheerleader in high school, and, may I say, eye candy. I'm sure she made her sales quotas.

Dr. Sax, your discussion of the Nucleus Accumbens being damaged by drugs was fascinating. There is more, though.

What happens to anything you eat? It goes into your stomach, to the intestines, and either "out with the trash", so to speak, or into the bloodstream. Fat soluble toxins are filtered out by the oil filter, aka the liver. Water soluble toxins are filtered out by the kidneys.

The liver stores toxins in the fat around it. If you start a fast, you may feel bad, at first, as the toxins are released from the fat being consumed. I have read that all cancer starts out with liver shutdown, due to having too many toxins. Something like over 200,000 new compounds are introduced into the environment, each year, with none of them being tested for toxicity.

I've read that some children now have larger livers, as bodies adapt to the massive numbers of new toxins in the environment. The average American home has more toxic chemicals in it than a Chemistry lab of 1900. Could that be one reason why the cancer rate of 1 in 25, in 1900, is now better than 1 in 3? Just maybe? Is this toxic load related to allergies?

All externally administered hormones cause cancer, I've read. One has only to read the package inserts. This includes the hormones in meat, and milk.

Drugs taken for a short time are one thing. Drugs taken for a long time are something else again. They are, basically, a toxic kind of food, doing something food should be doing. This is not any kind of medical opinion, or advice, it is an observation. Dr. Sax seems to have picked up on this- drugs taken for any length of time have other effects, that may not be very positive.

I have a friend, who grew up ADD. He was treated very badly, all through school. He calls ADD "CDD", or Culturally Deficient Disorder. It's not the kid who is messed up, it is our society. ADHD treatments are a Procrustean[23] bed, from his point of view.

---

23 There's something you don't see so much any more- a reference to Greek mythology, as the country dumbs down its education. Procrustes would take travellers, and put them in a bed. If their legs were too long, he would cut off their feet, to fit. If their feet were too short, he would

My friend works seven days per week, at his current job, and loves every minute of it. He has the ADHD frenzy that makes it possible for him to do a fantastic job, that no-one without it could do.

Native Americans had an honored place for ADD kids, and their training started as early as the age of five. Our culture prefers to throw them on the garbage heap of dysfunction and drug addiction.

Jared's story, at pp. 94-95, is right on. I was teased, also, for being a nerd. I didn't give up, though, I decided to live in defiance of those people. I insulted them right back, cut them deep to their core, and they learned to leave me alone.

I like the idea that it is possible to go off the medications, and blossom. I've met people who did this.

These kids are not "damaged goods", or if they are, it is due to the toxic load of diet and drugs, not some inherent problem. The book *Treehugger,* by Shamus Flaherty, tells the story of an ADD kid, grown up. He accomplished quite a bit of good. He was one of those guys with a criminal record as long as your arm. Now think about that- as long as your arm. This is someone with a lot of energy. How do we focus that energy on positive achievement?

These are the people with the energy to solve society's problems. Why aren't they being focused on that? Why do we spent up to $50,000/year housing and feeding them at government expense, in institutions, when they could be self-supporting, and curing society's problems? Native American elders ask those questions. Why aren't we?

---

stretch them on a rack. Those whose legs fit, had no problems. This is a metaphor for modern education. Do it my way, to my standards, or we drug you. Sounds like a nightmare Sci Fi movie, doesn't it? So many teachers have told me that the American educational system is set up with massive cracks, that so many students fall through.

Chapter 5: Endocrine disruptor issues

I was in Spain, and mentioned I was sometimes irritated by soy products, to a doctor. The doctor said I would do well to be very aware of labels. In Spain, dairy products are commonly used to bolster protein in food. In the U.S., soy products are used for this. I've read that soy products, also, can apparently function as endocrine disruptors, for boys.

I've heard people say that wheat allergies may be to the pesticides and other toxin residues on wheat, not to the wheat itself. Many pesticides are used on soybeans. You may want to ensure that you get organic soybeans, for this reason. Endocrine disruptors add to the toxic load.

A. Infertility and impotence

Dr. Sax mentions that many men in colleges and universities in the Washington, D.C. area, are impotent, and even losing interest in sex. There are male fish with eggs in their sex organs. I guess the people who wanted to make men androgynous succeeded beyond their wildest dreams.

Infertility is nature's way of telling a person that they have too many toxins in their system, to handle offspring. Roughly half of American men over 50 are impotent. Did you think a diet full of toxins might just be a factor?

The phthalates from plastic bottles are only one of the many new toxins in American diet. And, at p. 103, it is noted that nothing was done about this particular toxin. This is typical. ADHD is rare in India, and China. Yes. And they don't use the plastic bottles nearly as much.

Testosterone fuels a boy's drive to achieve, to be the best, to compete. The androgynizers hate testosterone. Gosh, they got their wish, with slackers.

B. Fat teenagers

Environmental estrogens, and bisphenol A, are no doubt a factor. The extremely high concentration of processed carbohydrates in today's diet is also a factor.

When I was in college, people got the "munchies". It took me some years to figure out why. If you eat food, which has little nutrition in it, your body keeps the hunger feeling on, to get more nutrition.

I learned this in wilderness skills classes. 2/3 cup per day, of wild foods, as in the books of Linda Runyon, is more than enough for a day. Eat any more, and it's as if you ate a Thanksgiving dinner. When the body gets the nutrition it needs, hunger shuts off.

American food is very non-nutritious. The body does what it can. America has been the fattest country in the world. Hey, Americans do well in competitions, right? America is number 1 in the world for colon cancer per capita, due in part to crummy diet, and toxin load. Go team!

C. Boys with fragile bones

Milk is not a very good source of calcium. Cow's milk is formulated to turn a calf into a 2,000 pound steer, quickly. It is also full of hormones, and phlegm. You will never see this in the media, because, pardon the pun, too many sacred cows would be hurt. I love dairy products, but I've had to cut them out of my diet, because they fill me with phlegm.

If you want calcium, there are other foods, notably sesame seeds, that are better. Minerals processed by plants are far, far more usable than those from other sources.

The book notes that environmental estrogens may be a factor in boys having more bone fractures than they used to. Dr. Sax notes that boys have more brittle bones now, at p. 11. This can be a sign of an acidic body chemistry. The phosphoric acid in many soft drinks dissolves bone, by changing tricalcium phosphate, which is not soluble in water, to dicalcium phosphate, which is soluble in water.

The people I see with fragile bones are invariably on an acidifying diet. Dr. Sax notes that boys drink more cola beverages, nowadays. These have the acidity of vinegar, with none of the positive effects.

The corn syrup alone makes me sick. I cannot drink anything with artificial sweeteners in it. I don't like the flavor of plastic soda, from plastic bottles, either. I notice that when I quit drinking soft drinks, I started feeling a lot better. Other people have told me the same thing. I have noticed that flashy packaging is usually a sign that the food it contains will make me feel bad.

Male reproductive problems, as at pp. 112-3, are growing. What is the media solution? Ignore them, till we can't have children any more. That is what happens, to infertile people. How many Shakers are left, for example?

The suggestion to avoid PVC's is great. Microwave ovens are best avoided, I don't trust them at all. To me, they kill off the life in food. I may have to tolerate microwaved food on a plane, but I don't eat it, normally. Food tastes much better, to me, if it is not microwaved.

D. Perhaps we could do regular detoxification?

Dr. Richard Schulze has a detox program, for helping the body to get rid of built up toxins. Every time I do it, I feel absolutely great. I get nothing for saying this. His is not the only detox protocol, of course.

With all the toxins in America, what about having a detox, say, once per season, at least in schools? The slackers are slackers, in part, due to built up toxins. You can easily test this. Eat garbage for a month. Oh wait, a guy did that, and made a movie about it. It is called *Supersize Me*, with Morgan Spurlock.

Everything Dr. Sax says is happening to boys happened to Morgan, when he ate only McDonald's food, for just one month. You see it all, right on the screen. The doctors he went to were telling him to go off the Micky D diet, immediately. He was also impotent, by the third week.

I quit eating food like that 20 years ago. I knew it then. Raul Molinas, the host of a Spanish language show on Univision, who is also a food critic, says that Subway is the only restaurant he will trust to feed his kids, on the road. I saw no evidence he was paid to say that. They probably use some chemicals, but far fewer than other chain restaurants.

I will normally only eat in small, family-owned restaurants, where I know the owners, and food is prepared fresh, every day. That kind of food tastes better, and I feel better eating it.

There is a restaurant chain in my part of the country, where the food tastes too good. One day it hit me- there is no way food frozen, and commercially prepared, as theirs was, could taste that way. I never entered their door again. The book *Fast Food Nation* notes that special chemicals are put in rancid food, to make it taste good. Just another addition to the toxic load, I guess.

There is a well-known Mexican food restaurant chain. Their food is made up in Mexico, deep frozen, and trucked here. It sits, frozen, for months. Have you heard of freezer burn? I wonder what chemicals they are putting in their food, to avoid that?

I worked in a fast food restaurant when I was in high school. The fat for the french fries came in large cubes- yes, solid cubes- which we melted down. The orange drink is all plastic.

I read labels now, carefully. I reject anything with cottonseed or canola oil. Both tend to be toxic, with lots of pesticide residues. I don't care what lies the media want to tell me, if these are on the food label, the product goes back on the shelf. I don't eat corn any more. It's all GMO. The fact that they won't label it tells me it's got to be horrible. We wouldn't have toxic food, if people weren't buying it.

I am in my 50's, with a healthy, energetic 5 year old daughter. Perhaps my detoxes, and diet of live foods, had something to do with it? I have more sex drive, and energy, now, than I did when I was 19. One reason is diet, and particularly, sprouts. Remember the old expression about wild oats? Eating live foods has an effect. Dr. John Christopher, and Paul Bragg's books talk about this, among others.

Maybe you have seen Jack LaLanne selling juicers, on infomercials. Jack was in extremely bad health, in his 20's, when he met Bragg. Bragg gave him some tips, on live food, and, well, he's selling juicers, more than a half century later[24].

If you want to energize a slacker, you could turn him on to freshly made juice, instead of plastic soda. Dr. Schulze told all of his clients, on their first visit, to get a juicer. If they didn't have it on the second visit, he threw them out of his office. 80% of the nutrition in juice is gone, an hour after it is made. Freshly made juice isn't really digested. When it hits the intestines, it goes right into the bloodstream.

I also have a Vitamix. I make fresh soups with it, in thirty seconds, for example. I use it every day. You don't see much about real health in the media, somehow. What is their incentive, again? To sell you products[25].

I recall that one of Dr. Schulze's 20 rules for health [for adults] is to have more sex. I'm good with that. The only sustainable way to do that is to detox, and eat healthy, live food that fills you with energy. Drugs are not the answer. Viagra kills people. How many drugs have they had to ban, after it was found they were dangerous?

Nobody seems to have put together toxic load, and birth defects. I wonder why? Perhaps because those who profit from the toxic load have no interest in connecting the dots. Do you really think the two can be unrelated, though?

I wonder what connection there is, between demineralized, unhealthy soils, and plants having to be goosed with artificial fertilizers, and poisons, just to grow? Maggots are sometimes used by doctors, as they will only eat dead flesh.

---

24 I used to enjoy Jay the Juicer. He was about 70, with white hair. He had a 30 year old wife, and two sons, about 10 and 11. Yeah! Juice! I have fresh juice every day. Thanks Jay!

25 I heard a community organizer say that the mass media wants to fill you with fear, distrust for your neighbor, to keep you away from healthy community activities, so you will be alone, lonely, and sick- and buy more products, to try to fill the void that only healthy interaction with other people, in a healthy community, can fill. He said they don't sell you as many products, if you are eating healthy food, fresh juice, interacting in a healthy way with people, and enjoying life. I don't know if that's true.

Insects generally don't attack healthy plants. They attack weak, diseased plants, plants getting poor nutrition. They are nature's way of culling weak plants, just as predators cull weak prey animals.

Truly healthy food plants, grown in compost, organically, in a healthy way, do not need pesticides, or artificial fertilizers. Their immune system naturally rejects pests. When their immune systems are impaired, due to lousy diet, they have problems, and need drugs, pesticides, and so on. The toxic load begins with how our food plants are grown.

Meat has a lot of penicillin, and other antibiotics, in it. The reason is that in feedlots, diseases would be rampant, without it. Cows and chickens can live their entire lives, without ever seeing the sun, surrounded by manure, and urine. They are packed together, densely.

Perhaps one reason Boys Adrift prefer to stay indoors, under artificial lighting, not getting exercise, is that they are eating the flesh of animals, who lived their lives in the same way?

Slaughterhouses are interesting, too. Animals know what is to happen, for a few hours prior. I wonder what kind of fear hormones are released, into their flesh? What do animals in terror for their lives feel, I wonder?

I don't watch slasher movies. I would observe, however, that they seem to re-enact exactly what an animal in a slaughterhouse would feel. Perhaps the hormones in meat train those who eat that meat, to enjoy this kind of entertainment? You are what you eat.

A TV station secretly filmed how a grocery chain, Food Lion, was doctoring rotten meat, to remove the smell, and appearance of being rotten. They aired it. Instead of correcting the problem, Food Lion sued them. I quite eating grocery store meat that day. Do you really think other grocery chains aren't doing exactly the same thing? And what media outlet will ever cover that again, with that example of what happens when they do?

Chapter 6: Failure to Launch

There is no failure to launch. American culture has been working to androgynize boys, for more than thirty years. It worked. Androgyny has been launched. Actions have consequences. We have a culture full of slackers, not by accident, but by design.

A. Respect is an incentive

Dr. Sax's book notes the difficulties in getting students for the trades. I'm not sure the example of plumbers is entirely valid. In Spain, they call people who work at manual trades "monos", ostensibly from the one-piece uniforms they sometimes wear. Mono also means "monkey", in Spanish.

In Spain, there is no respect for the manual trades whatsoever, no matter how well paid. If you want respect, in Spain, as a man, you must be in a job that requires you to wear suit and tie, to work, even if the tie is tied loosely, to reduce the wear on it, so it will last longer.

The disrespect for manual trades in the U.S. is not quite as focused, but it's there, as noted at p. 122. That is relevant. The lack of energy among apprentices, in the trades, that Dr. Sax cites, is, to me, typical of people with an acidic body chemistry.

The native Alaskan who could hear a sea lion approaching at five miles is not unusual, for indigenous peoples. They often had sensory acuity beyond what Western people can imagine. Fifty years ago, they had men's houses, in Alaska, slightly larger than sweat houses, where the art of hunting was passed on.

But the missionaries destroyed the houses. Grocery stores made getting food easier, though food quality went down. Weston Price's profound book on what white man food does to teeth is an example of this.

So now the young men of the island lack mission and purpose, in their lives. They end up incarcerated, alcoholic, addicts, or dead from suicide. P. 126 notes that this is true in many other places, in Alaska.

It is also true in America's inner cities, isn't it[26]?

There was a time when the man was the primary provider, first by hunting, then by agriculture, then by wage work. Women stayed home, mostly. My grandmother did laundry on Monday- by hand, with a washboard, and buckets; ironing on Tuesday, with a flatiron- electric irons weren't available until later; mending on Wednesday, baking on Thursday.

There were no mixes, and bulk items like coffee, flour, and sugar were sold out of barrels, and put in paper bags. My parents used an expression- "now you're cooking with gas!", which reflects how welcome gas ovens were, to people who cooked with wood, or coal.

During the Civil War, women in Confederate states actually took looms and spinning wheels out of attics, to make homespun cloth. Women were an irreplaceable contribution to the household, then. I doubt we will ever go back to that, short of a significant catastrophe that puts us back into 19th century technology.

But men do need a place. What is the media's answer? Househusbands. Great. Men taking over child care, housecleaning, laundry, cooking? Uhh, no, it's not happening, mostly. How many societies were there, where the men did this, historically?

Women left it because they felt it had no status[27]. Men won't go into fields with no status, usually. A very few have, and they end up in the newspapers. You know, yesterday 99.999999999999999999% of the world's population had a pretty good day. But that's not what you'll see in the media. The media distorts perception.

As Dr. Sax points out, stay-at-home dads don't vacuum, do laundry, make meals, clean, or take care of the children, not for any length of time. If you look back on history, the family household has been pretty stable. We are losing it, in this country. Daniel Patrick Moynihan noted the effect of rising percentages of single parent households among minorities, in the 1960's. Now other groups are going this way. The new forms are not as stable, are they. Society is also not as stable.

---

26 It's not a Gangsta's Paradise, it's a Feminist's Paradise. Dr. Sax can't say that. I can.

27 Listen to the hatred poured on Dr. Laura, if you doubt this.

B. Another kind of video game

My father told me that you could get anything you wanted, from women, outside of marriage, except a stable environment for raising kids. That was in the 1970's. Do we want a stable, supportive environment for raising children? I'm not sure Americans do, based on their actions.

Pornography has grown and grown. Needing Viagra, or Cialis, because of porn overuse is just sad. I see young girls in outfits prostitutes would have been ashamed to wear, thirty years ago. But that's where modern fashions come from, nowadays. First the prostitutes, then Madonna or Britney, then the gays, then it's high fashion, then it's mass market, then it's discounted, then it's out of fashion. They used to call this seriation, in college, super-imposed sine waves, on a graph, as trends go up and down[28].

It is easy to criticize porn. Yet women have their own. One version of it is called Romance Novels. 40% of books in print are Romance Novels[29]. How bad is a culture, when both genders have to have fantasy like this? In most Muslim countries, Romance novels are considered porn, and punished accordingly. They judge by the cover, and probably don't read much of the text, but the covers are lurid enough[30].

I have never heard of a magazine, or video, suing any guy for child support, or alimony. I prefer real food, however, occasionally the cooking magazine, and video cooking show, could be of use, at times.

I have looked at the plastic ladies in *Playboy,* or used to. I know they are pure fantasy. Not all men do. Years ago, I worked as a security guard, at a time when Playboy centerfolds could still be posted in the workplace.

---

28 Why is all that pornfashion necessary? Could it be that people have such a high toxic load, that they have to overcompensate? Dr. Schulze notes that teenagers don't need toys, or special costumes, like some adults, they just go at it. What role is toxic load playing here?

29 Women's porn is available in any bookstore, but men's is considered bad, and is regulated. Is this a double standard? I'm just asking.

30 In Saddam Hussein's Iraq, each pornographic picture earned for its owner 6 months in jail. The men have no real outlet. It results in an energy flow which is interesting. I knew an Arab student, in college. All he had to do was look at a woman, the right way, and she wanted to sleep with him, and did so, on request. So he took his college courses from female professors. I wouldn't have believed it, had I not seen it for myself. Some Italian and French men, particularly, can also do this.

One guy I was training looked at the centerfold, and wished he could meet a woman like that. I explained to him that this would never happen. No woman ever looked like that, in the history of the world, and none ever would.

I explained to him that he was getting excited about an image that was 80% paint, applied with an airbrush. The understanding dawned in his face, and he understood. I love it when people get enlightened, even on small things. I wonder if his later girlfriends knew that he appreciated them more, because he was no longer comparing them to a fantasy image. Nowadays it would be Photoshop, of course.

A Native American was discussing traditional warrior training, for his people. He said the trainees had no time for *Playboy*, or anything like that. Hmm. The word Playboy. What does that mean? Isn't that kind of like... a slacker? It certainly has slacker ideas about sex.

The books cited on raunch culture were right on, Dr. Sax. Raunch culture seems to reflect a serious lack of self-respect.

C. Duty

My parents were of the WW II generation. They believed in duty, and they lived it. My father put up with crummy jobs, at times. John Wayne's roles were mostly that of a flawed character, who somehow did his duty. Jimmy Stewart was a bomber captain, in a war where 10% of aviators died in combat. He could have stayed, safe, in Hollywood. He never would do a war movie, afterwards, though. I think about that, when I see *It's a Wonderful Life.*

What kind of heroes do we have now, though? Do we even have heroes? I saw the Iron Man character, arguing with Captain America, on one of those Avengers movies. The Iron Man character, played by Robert Downey, Jr., I think, had a more modern, selfish viewpoint, while Captain America, who was an adult in the 1940's, had a more duty focused viewpoint. I find more truth in movies made for kids, than those made for adults. They seem deeper, also.

It was an interesting contrast. I favored Captain America's arguments more. Gwyneth Paltrow does look good in a sports bra, though, I had to agree with Iron Man on that. I remember training a guy, for a job, some years ago. I spent a day training him. He never showed up again[31].

My first wife ran away with my best friend, and left our young daughter with me. I got custody. I had to abandon my career path, to my ideal job, and take another job that would allow me to take care of her.

It wasn't easy. She was rebellious, at times. My family has never abandoned its children, and I knew it wasn't going to start with me. I was harassed in the Army, for that. I heard "The Army didn't issue you that child, why do you have it?" "We aren't going to cut you any slack, just because you are a single parent."

In her senior year of high school, she decided to live with her mother. This turned out to be a blessing. She got to see her mother as she truly was. She could appreciate that I had invested a lot in her. She actually sent me a letter of apology, when she was in college, for the trouble she'd given me. I guess she saw some hardcases, with no parents, or really abusive parents.

I met her recently. She is a joy. She embodies my values better than I do. She knows what duty is, because she saw her father doing his. Duty is simply doing unpleasant things now, for the greater good. It is something only mature adults do.

D. Slackers who fail to launch

There were plenty of slackers, when I was in college, even the college I went to, which wasn't a party school. Most had new cars. Most had female or male guests over, at least on weekends. Most had their choice of drugs. Invariably, they were the sons and daughters of the rich.

I know a guy who was in a prep school, in Massachusetts. There was a guy in his class who was a total idiot. No-one listened to him.

---

31 Duty is doing what needs to be done, even though you don't want to do it. For example, I have gotten up at 2 hour intervals, to feed a newborn, and gone to work, tired, for years at a time. It wasn't fun. I lived in a hospital for three weeks, with a newborn daughter, because my wife couldn't do it, as she was sick.

His parents were rich, and he knew he didn't have to work in school. His name was Jeb Bush, the bright one of the Bush brothers. George boasted about making C's. So slackers can get to be president. The children of the rich are slackers, in many parts of the world. There are slackers in Russia. I read about one, the son of well-connected parents. He had all the vodka, drugs, luxury goods, and beautiful women he wanted.

Dunstan, the younger son of the rich family, in *Silas Marner,* was a slacker, come to think of it... and you thought I didn't pay attention in class.

E. Response to the messages

Yogabody125 is cited at p. 137, as being a 35 year old woman, with her own house, car, and career. The single men she meets still live with their parents, or else they are still deciding what to do with their lives. This has happened a lot, she says[32].

OK, Yogabody. You state you are 35. My mother was 30 when she got married, and that was considered long in the tooth, back then. Yes, we live in a different world. The responsible men you seek marriage with, in your age range, are, mostly, already tied up, in marriage. Those that aren't may not want to be married, or even to be involved with you. They may have better options.

If you want to find a responsible man, who wants to marry you, you may need to find a divorced man, or an older man, who hasn't been totally turned off to women. I can only say, may Allah grant you patience, because you'll need the patience of an easterner. Men in their 20's are stupid. Pain brings them wisdom, and by their late 20's, they are starting to wake up. When they hit 35, they are much more aware.

---

32 American career women often seem to have an image in their mind, that they will find a man who makes more than they do, who will sweep them off their feet like the actors in soap operas, a fantasy figure available totally on their terms. A genie would be more realistic. The few men who might meet their fantasy specifications are making enough money that they don't want the lockdown of marriage. When they do decide to get married, they want a woman in Yin polarity, not Yang, generally. American women have the idea that they can be super-bitchy, and their soulmate fantasy man will see their true nature under that, and love them despite their bitchiness. Really be aware of this, in full consciousness. Who wants to put up with that?

You are apparently in the D.C. Area. The female to male ratio is high there. Marriage is becoming a worse and worse deal, for men. More and more men are only taking the best deals, and passing up the ok deals, for marriage. Are you the best deal? I mean, really?[33]

What are you really looking for? You have a house, a car, a career. You are Barbie, and the only accessory you lack is Ken. Oh wait, you have that, too, the 25 year old "boy toy" you cite, that you put away when you are done playing with. You have all the accessories. Why are you complaining, again?

Anna M. is 24, with a boyfriend of over six years. His mother does his laundry, meals, bed, and so on. What on earth did you stay with a slacker like this for? And you're moving in with him this summer? Huh? What's wrong with this picture? Who is more the fool, the fool, or the fool that follows the fool?

Sarah C. is 25, with a "boy" of 29. You make twice what he does. His family still tries to bail him out. You clearly have no respect for him, though you state you love him.

---

33 Instead of seeing a static world, can we understand that we are part of interlocking systems? In the natural world, prey animals learn and apply camouflage, stealth, strategy, and so on, as predators do the same. Many prey animals are never seen by predators, due to stealth. I have had to use stealth, notably in the military. Do women really think smarter men, especially above the age of 27-30, aren't using stealth? That smarter men aren't intuiting danger, and sidestepping it? This is even before we consider the filtering effect of belief systems. People find confirmation for their belief systems, and they don't see what they don't expect to see. Slackers exist, just as deer exist. I've talked to deer hunters, who realized that the smarter deer were aware of them, despite their excellent camouflage, which was quite sufficient for less smart deer. One hunter noted that the smarter deer even enjoyed stealthily sneaking up on him, shocking him, and then getting away before he could even think of getting a shot off. One of Tom Brown, Jr.'s instructors remembered being with a friend, in the woods, seeing a huge buck deer, and pantomiming shooting the deer, with an imaginary rifle. He was otherwise disrespectful to the woods. They had no weapons with them. The buck paid them a visit that night. He straddled the disrespecter's sleeping bag, and emptied his bladder on it, soaking it through. The buck ignored the other guy. Maybe this is why Native Americans hunted only out of respect? Asking the deer which one wanted to die, to feed the people? Maybe the smarter men are staying in the shadows of the perception of these women, for safety? I know I can assume the roles of a totally unaware nerd, a gay, a slacker, a brain, and others, to evade a woman. Further, sometimes these roles come up without my consciously summoning them. After I review events, I realize they came up to protect me from a situation. This is basic Ninjitsu, for that matter. So many American women seem to assume that all men are as stupid as teenagers, and can be easily manipulated. Such women do not attract those men who have no desire or need to learn in that school. If there are deer smart enough to evade and fool humans, don't you think there might be men that are smart enough to avoid bitchy vampiresses? Those who would do the impossible must learn to see the invisible.

Women wanted to have all their options open, and now you know how a good number of married men feel. Only they are more trapped than you are.

Rachel Riggs says girls today feel they don't need boys so much. Gosh, how about that. How does it feel, I wonder, to not be needed? Since they can't be a hero to their girlfriends, or wives, they can at least be so with video games. Sleeping around. Gosh, who made that so easy? Oh, wait, you satisfy yourself in that aspect. Cool. I guess you're all set.

Clearly you don't need a man. And then you say that what if women decide that they've had enough of men, their huge egos, and testosterone-fueled wars... First of all, the wars nowadays happen to enrich armaments companies. Guess who gets to fight those wars? Mostly men.

Yes, I know combat arms were recently opened to women, but I've been in the Army. Women were never expected to operate at the same level as the male soldiers, ever, anywhere[34]. War is not fun. More Vietnam veterans have committed suicide than died in Vietnam. The VA, and Congress, couldn't care less about veterans. I know- I see it. They'll speak their BS on Veteran's Day, but that's it.

And now you want to stockpile frozen sperm until you don't need men any more? Feminists talk like this. First of all, animals that are products of artificial insemination die young, and aren't as healthy. It doesn't matter, since they are slaughtered young, though, as nobody notices. There are genetic problems with frozen sperm. Yes, I know, the media will never say it, the clinics that charge for artificial insemination won't ever tell you that, but it's true. If you can get a cattle rancher to trust you, you will learn much. Food loses a lot, when frozen, over time. Think about freezer burn. Why would sperm be any different[35]?

---

34 Some did, out of self-respect. But they didn't have to. And they don't now, despite the lies that the commander of TRADOC recently put out.

35 There is a spiritual side to this, also. Look at anyone you like. Really feel their energy. Now ask yourself, How much in love were their parents, when they were conceived? The intuitive answer I get has always proven true, when I could check it. That is not measurable with lab instruments, but nonetheless real. I know people whose parents were very much in love, and I know others whose parents weren't. I notice a major qualitative difference.

You are divorced, and you miss a male presence. The world would be a worse place without men, you say. Women are evolving, and men are reacting. I couldn't agree more with this. This is what happens in any environmental system. Let's talk about that male reaction.

Many men are scared of divorced women. I know single men, in their 50's and 60's, who go out with women from the personal ads. They tell me they avoid divorced women. Widows, they say, are usually fine, but divorced women always have a sharp edge to them.

For a man, sensing that edge, in a divorced woman, feels kind of like finding a good used car, at a great price, and then suddenly noticing water damage, because the car was a "flood car", totally submerged in water for a time, which means it won't last long. Oh, wait, I can't ask you to see yourself from the perspective of men, that might be sexist. Forget I said that.

Sharon S says, at 29, that her generation is the middle of failure to launch, at p. 142. Really? My daughter is 29, and she got married this year, to a great guy. She met him two towns out from Annapolis, which isn't far from Northern Virginia, is it? The guy works unbelievably hard, is successful, and is really bright. He is polite, respectful, and I can't think of any downside to him.

She was dating his friend, also single and looking for a wife, also hardworking, with a real career, when she met him. She dumped a controlling boyfriend two years ago- an engineer, of her age, who went on to get engaged to another woman. All of them are in your generation.

What you say could be correct. I believe what you say is also due to sampling bias. You say you are newly divorced, and there just aren't any worthwhile men out there[36]. This is a transparent belief system[37], which filters your experience. For a time, I believed there were no worthwhile women out there, and none showed up. When I realized the error in my thinking, I cleaned that out. Worthwhile women showed up.

---

36 Perhaps you are simply attracting men who mirror back your own beliefs about men? P. 126, *Calling in "The One"*, Katherine Woodward Thomas, New York: Three Rivers Press, 2004.
37 What we don't bring into consciousness appears in our lives as fate. -Carl Jung

You say you'd rather be on your own, than with a man who can't stand on his own. No, you'd rather be alone, and you have created this for yourself, very effectively. Results are the only report card.

Allie, at p. 143, is 28, and has noticed that she and her friends are talking about how relationships with the 30 year old little boys around them impedes successful careers, and having children. If you can't find what you want, you'll adopt, or find some other way of having children.

I can feel women like you at a distance of 30 meters. I find my subconscious making me invisible to women like you, sometimes outside of any conscious intention on my part. I know guys in my nephew's generation- he is 28- who do this, also. Toxic judgment like this feels painful, to me. I have nothing to prove to women like this, except how fast I can evade them, and stay under their radar.

Your view of these men is similar to how feminists view men. Could there be a belief system filter, in your thinking? If you say "all the good ones are taken", then they will be[38].

Maxine C. cites her boyfriend as having called off the wedding. He's a teacher with a Master's. Now you're glad he backed out. You own your own home. Welcome to the real world. Sometimes what seems painful is for our best good.

Penny, at p. 145, says the men staying at home phenomena is a reaction to the feminist era. The massive amount of disrespect thrown at responsible men, which still continues, probably did have an effect, Penny[39].

---

38 P. 157, *Calling in "The One"*, Katherine Woodward Thomas, New York: Three Rivers Press, 2004.
39 My father taught me to cultivate black people, and Jews. He said that people who could survive what used to thrown at them always had useful lessons. Black people, and Jews, had to make themselves invisible, also, sometimes just to stay alive. Responsible men are ridiculed, and dissed, as much as black people and Jews used to be, I've noticed, and it's not just feminists. If Homer Simpson was black, in blackface, how long would that show have lasted, on TV? Why would any man want to commit to a relationship that costs a lot of energy to maintain, under the best of circumstances, with the additional burden of major disrespect, major risk of economic devastation, and even unprovoked attacks? If I want to understand someone, I walk into them, and feel what they feel. American women seem to be getting more and more materialistic, and less and less aware. They don't seem to understand that selling their physical assets is selling what economists call a wasting asset, that declines in value, or that developing themselves spiritually not only increases their value, it opens them up to a much nicer life. But maybe that's my perceptual

Some men want to marry you because you are a lawyer, you say? Wow. They've never been divorced, I guess. Divorced men I know would wear garlic, get a holy water squirtgun, and make the sign of the cross, if they thought they were near a female lawyer.

Feminists opened up opportunities for women, and men, and they weren't all so nice. It's different when the shoe is on the other foot, isn't it? My second wife openly told my mother she married me for my paycheck, and medical insurance. Men get this all the time, even now. It makes you feel really special, to be exploited in this way, doesn't it?

Aliya Husain, at p. 145, notes that children live with their parents in adulthood, in every other country. They do this in Spain, and Latin countries. The older generation is revered, unlike in this country. Aliya, it may be that the corporations fostered this kind of disrespect for the old, because the old give good advice, which causes their children to be wiser, and spend less money.

You say that kids living with parents can create disincentives to work. True. I liked your letter. I've always enjoyed foreigners, because they tend to see the world more clearly. Your letter is the most realistic one in the bunch.

Richard R. is male, 27, married, and in grad school. He notes that games give a sense of beauty to those who can't find it in their physical world. This is useful- beauty is food for the soul. I had no time for games, in grad school, myself.

WhatisanAdult notes that he picks up more pretty girls than he can count. They used to say why buy the cow, when milk is so cheap, when my parents were young[40]. Dr. Sax says the motivation to have a family and career is service, and meaning in life. FUN at some point loses its punch.

I've seen guys just like him to, all of a sudden, decide to dump the good times girls, and go out and get married[41]. The worst sinner makes the best saint, as the old proverb goes.

---

bias; maybe I have some filters to clear.
40 My grandfather bought the cow, and was happy with what he had.
41 But only very rarely to the good times girls.

This is an observation about polarity, and energy shifts.

Mike, at p. 152, notes that he had a string of dead end jobs. Do you think the pot, video games, and beer might have been a part of that, Mike? Oh wait, you say yourself, beer and pot sapped your energy. They do that. The only way to get anywhere is to cut those off, now, completely.

Mike Cleveland, at p. 157, notes that the military draft ended in the 70's. My father's generation didn't like the military, but the WW II generation was very, very disciplined. I knew a WW II veteran, who was working in his 80's. He was very, very good at his job.

Mike says the threat of being drafted encouraged young men to do well in college. This may be true. I note that some of the slackers of back then went into the military, and thrived. This includes Special Forces, and Navy SEALS.

Mary W, at p. 159, talks of a 26 year old son who dropped out of Northwestern after one year. His father passed on when he was 20. Mary, men at the age of 30 or so start focusing on their careers. What they do before then is one thing. If you can get him into martial arts classes, or wilderness skills schools, anything to get him out of the comfortable nest he's in now, that could help.

Sometimes just getting people to talk drains out their built up feelings, because Americans generally don't get listened to, much. Getting an older man to help him drain out might help, also, if you can arrange it. I've done this, on request, for people I trust.

Kent Robertson notes that some grown men, when their marriage fails, drift towards zero ambition, in pursuit of personal gratification, exploiting every sexual opportunity. That's true, Kent.

The movie *It's a Wonderful Life* shows a little bit of the many, many concentric rings one person's actions send out. Marriage is healthy, when it's calibrated properly, for all participants. The Chinese say that as the family goes, so goes society. The Chinese understand fractal energy.

The love of a good woman, and ambitions for family, may well be the engine that runs society at least, if not the world[42]. Kent, a good woman, a wife, is like a power source, for a man. I've seen men in great marriages who had far more energy, as a direct result of the relationship they had with their wives. Napoleon Hill even talks about this. And it is good for the wives, in the same way. My Aunt Betty outlived all of her siblings, because she had a great marriage.

F. Why the house doesn't matter

I knew a divorced guy in his late 50's. He went out with a 32 year old woman, who owned her own house, and had 3 kids. She wanted a father for her children. He passed it up. What does that tell you? She wasn't finding guys in her own age range. It tells you something else. The fact she had a house didn't do a lot for him. Since so many women cited this, in Dr. Sax's book, we'll talk about it.

Men know that choosing the wrong woman can cripple them economically. But there's more. If you made much more money than the man you were dating, and told him that, you'd think he'd relax. Uhh, no, unless he's only interested in your money. Women can have gaps on their resume, for children, long vacations, whatever. Men can't; well, they can't, and hope to get good jobs. And, American women, nowadays, can and do walk out of a marriage any time they feel like it, which means men have to have something to fall back on.

Maybe you make ten times what the man makes. You offer him money. He'll usually turn it down. He may have to eat bagel lunches till payday, but he won't take it.

A responsible man knows that if he gets dependent on money other than what he makes, he might turn into... a slacker. If a man isn't confident he can provide for a family by himself, he may not even consider the prospect of marriage[43], no matter how wealthy a potential mate might be. Men identify with their jobs.

---

42 *Men and Marriage,* George Gilder, NY: Pelican Publishing, 1992, discusses this at length.
43 Pp. 135-7, *Why Men Fear Marriage*, R.M. Johnson, New York: Simon and Schuster, 2009.

Men know they are losers long before anyone else does. Video games may ease the pain, but they know it, deep down, no matter how much denial they put out. A man can eat pork and beans, and ramen noodles, and sleep on the floor, by himself, with the thermostat on 40, but having family- dependents- is different.

Imagine the wife saying, "You're the man of the house, and you can't even find a job." That cuts deep, even to the slackers, but they won't show it. Women do not understand that men won't show pain. My wife asks me why I don't tell her when I'm hurting. I tell her that when I was in school, if you let on you were hurting, they just made it worse.

Do you remember the story about the Spartan boy, who hid the fox in his coat? And let the fox eat out his stomach, and fell dead to the ground, instead of letting it show? I've seen men in denial like that, who wouldn't show even the worst of pain.

Successful women know to not disclose they own a home too soon, because men don't take it well[44]. One man visited his girlfriend, in her house. Ten minutes after entering, he said he wasn't the right guy for her. Why? It's very simple. It wasn't intimidation. It was a man avoiding being put in a one-down position, with less power than the woman.

Let's imagine that points were given for salary, education, experience, job title, and so on. Men really do this. One man was married to a woman who had more points than he did, in every category. He also lived in her home. This woman would criticize him for not washing the dishes right, and so on. Wow.

Was he her husband, or manservant? Black men may call this the woman having the man wear the panties. The homeowner is the ruler. Men know this, in their guts. That man left the marriage, too. Why put up with disrespect? It only gets worse. A woman who owns her own house can say, "If you don't like it, get out of MY house.[45]" Most men have no interest in being in this position.

---

44 P. 149, *Why Men Fear Marriage*, R.M. Johnson, New York: Simon and Schuster, 2009.
45 P. 150, *Why Men Fear Marriage*, R.M. Johnson, New York: Simon and Schuster, 2009.

A man living in an apartment may avoid getting serious with a woman who has a house, or who otherwise one-ups him. Yang repeals Yang. I had a friend, whose mother was constantly setting him up with successful, smart Jewish women, just like her. He had no interest whatsoever. No, he wanted to choose the woman, and the house, and didn't feel like being controlled.

Part of being smart is avoiding bad situations. What is it like to have a woman in control? Many women have told me they much preferred male bosses. Female bosses- women tell me- are insecure, bitchy, unpredictable, blow up for no reason, make unreasonable demands, have unclear expectations, frequently find fault, and are generally very unpleasant to work for. This is women talking! Women have plenty of control in relationships as it is, even before one considers how the legal system is totally biased to favor them.

G. Does a woman really need a man?

What do women say, after about the age of 30 or so? I don't need a man[46]! This is followed by the male-bashing that women do in company[47]. OK, you've known men who played around, who were disrespectful. You don't want that man. Does this mean all men are bad? Does it? Barbara De Angelis calls this baggage. It weighs you down[48]. What if this was simply a lesson, in the largest school, life?

I had two wives that played around. Does that make all women bad? It doesn't. It just means I chose badly, based on inadequate perception, and calibration.

---

46 P. 159, *Why Men Fear Marriage*, R.M. Johnson, New York: Simon and Schuster, 2009. I don't hear men saying they don't need women. They say they don't need bossy, bitchy, moody, catty, frigid, unfocused women, but I can't recall ever hearing a man say he didn't need women.

47 I listen to women talk. Many American women have absolutely no respect whatsoever for their husbands. How do I know this? I listen to them talk, I watch their body language. For a man, considering a decision that could wipe him out, financially, how well does the no respect thing work?

48 *The Magic of Thinking Big*, by David Schwartz, tells a story about two men driving to meet a client. They spent an hour dissing the client, agreeing he was fatter than a cow, a total idiot, and so on. This builds an energy load. That client terminated their contract. Fat, male, unaware, and so on, he could feel the energy load. Do women really think men don't notice a similar energy load?

I scan everybody in a room, in public. On the street, I scan out 40-50 meters. When I scan a woman, and find that attitude, a sort of mental yellow warning tape is placed around her, with an imaginary sign to avoid her at all costs, and to say as little as possible to her[49]. I don't need to do this consciously, any more. It just happens, now.

I have two classifications, yellow, and red. Threat Level Red means avoid at all costs, go to stealth mode, and speak only if spoken to[50]. Any talk of feminism, by way, is an automatic Threat Level Red, for me. I know other men do this, also[51].

What does that mean? It means that often, I don't even need to think, as protective energy comes around me. I am guided, intuitively, to do whatever keeps me on low visibility to that woman. I don't even want to be in her Universe. I want to phase conjugate or scramble any attraction she might have to me, before I even deal with her.

H. Great products sell themselves

You are always selling yourself, when you deal with others. When you hear women complaining about the horrible men in their lives, you want to think about this. A great product sells itself- but must be sought out, with intent.

---

49 Here's an example. I knew a divorced single mother, who radiated hatred for men, like this. I put the yellow tape around her, and stayed away. She came up and asked me, in a public place, one day, for advice for her son, about the FBI. I recommended John Douglas' book, which is great. I have a rule, that I help people if I can. I also offer books to people, that feed their interests. People know this. I offered her a book, in a public place, for her son, saying if she didn't want it, that was fine. She looked at me as if I was hitting on her, with contempt. I have a big wedding ring, and I don't play around. No hay problema. Cool. I never talked to her again. Ever. I upgraded her to Threat Level Red. I told my wife about her, also. And, new rule: I give no more books to Threat Level Yellow people, even if they ask for help, no matter how strongly I feel about always helping people.

50 I scanned a guy in a restaurant, who didn't feel right. I got the distinct image of a hit-man. I gave him a wide berth, and went immediately into stealth mode, without even thinking. This was unmistakable Threat Level Red.

51 Think about why. What was it like, for black people, in the Old South, to wonder about whites- was this one a Christian, with a real heart, who at least wouldn't hurt them? Was this one a Church Christian, who had little use for black people? Was this one a Triple K-er? How do you tell? You can't. So you set up default classifications, like "avoid this group". Not all poisonous snakes bite, but does that mean you want to play with one? Black people did exactly what I am talking about.

A bad product requires manipulative salespeople, but it comes to you. Why would these women be surrounded by manipulative salespeople, selling inferior product [i.e. low grade, manipulative men- slackers, say]? Could it be they ignored, or drove away the superior product? This is called Gresham's Law, in economics. They probably don't know they did it. Or don't want to admit it.

If a woman wants a partner, to fall in love, marry, have healthy children, and raise them in partnership, gosh, maybe she might just need a man? Well, maybe not. She could marry a lesbian, in some states. But you know, lesbians also sometimes inflict domestic violence, or exploit their partners, in fact there are lesbians who do all the bad things some men do[52]. There is risk in dealing with anyone.

So you bought the house. Good. You can write off the interest, it's an investment, and so on. It is not an investment, when you hold it as a reason why men are insane to not be flooding the street up to the door for you. So you tell your female friends that you are thirty something, and have your own house. You don't want the men still living with their mothers[53].

There you are. Then something breaks, and you don't know what to do. Your mother would have asked your father to fix it. Well, you're liberated, you get a book from the library, and figure out how to fix it[54].

---

52 Many years ago, I was in a job where there was a horribly lazy lesbian, who couldn't be touched because management was afraid she'd sue. She put a solid hour of work in, some days, and was paid for eight. Other people, mostly women, had to pick up her work. She got a girlfriend, who was a total leach, I mean, pure vampire. I wouldn't want to say that I engaged in Schadenfreude, but I do know what the word means. There is no justice, but there is balance.

53 P. 166, *Why Men Fear Marriage*, R.M. Johnson, New York: Simon and Schuster, 2009. I'm not the only one putting this stuff in print, and this way you know that other men really do think this way. You won't find a lot of it in print, though. Men just put up with abuse. Few write.

54 The feminist landlady of a house I lived in had two of her lesbian friends come over, to do some repairs. They were very proud of how they fixed the heating system, and told me they didn't need any man to help them. I can keep a poker face. I'm smart enough not to insult people to their faces, so I don't say things like that, but what the heck, maybe there was some learning here. Uhh, yes. They forgot to tighten the pipes. When the heating system kicked in, we had 3 feet of fog, on the ceiling. Water and drywall don't go together well. My mother could fix things, very well, it's not like there aren't women who can fix things. That landlady wasn't very bright. She made the mistake of getting caught DWI, three times. They invited her to a free stay at the Greystone Hotel, courtesy of the state, for that. She was divorced, from a man, too. I wonder how he celebrated that, and I'm sure he thanked his Creator daily he never had a kid with her. I calibrated her carefully, so I could pick out women like her quickly, and do mental quarantine on sight, or before. There are some very bright lesbians out there, also, by way. The vice president of the Union I

Or not.

I. Bicycles are more stable than unicycles

Then, you go to bed. Only it's tough to sleep. You need to release some of the orgone energy that's piled up. You reach in to get Plastic Man- Mr. V, or is it Mr. Hitachi. After some days, though, his lovemaking style wears thin[55].

Maybe you call to get a plumber in, or maybe you are out in the world. Something happens. Maybe you find the salesman, with the inferior goods, at the singles bar[56]. You do the wild thing with him. It's mechanical.

Or maybe you find a charming guy, like the last one who dumped you. You rush into a relationship, introduce him to the family, start planning the wedding- and he backs out, because you're moving too fast. So you're hurt. You let the scar tissue form[57].

Instead of setting up positive filters, to filter out what you don't want, you settled for the first thing that came along, and it didn't work out. Guess what. There are a lot of guys who feel the same way.

---

belong to is by far the brightest leader we have. Do I care that she's lesbian? No. I help her any way I can. The allies who don't wear your uniform may be the most important allies you have.

55 P. 167, *Why Mean Fear Marriage,* R.M. Johnson, New York: Simon and Schuster, 2009.

56 Brett Butler did a marvelous routine on Bill Clinton being like the guy a woman finds, just before the bar closes, when she really doesn't want to go home alone. She asks, "Are you married?" and he says, "Now you know, I'm really glad you asked me that. This is an important question, and it deserves to be answered properly..." at which point the woman interrupts, and says, "Never mind, I'll go home with you."

57 American women have it better than 95% of women worldwide. In Brazil, a man can beat a woman to a pulp. The police do nothing, as long as he doesn't kill her. Oh, wait, in Muslim, and South American countries, a man can say a woman was sleeping around, and then kill her, largely with impunity. Seeing feminists, in college, complain mightily about domestic violence, and sexist men, and so on, as they scared away even the nerds, and then settling for third world men, was totally amusing to me and my friends. They would talk about having to understand their culture, and so on. Really? What was that movie, *Not Without my Daughter,* with Sally Field? About a woman married to an Iranian, who got out of Iran, because she discovered that promises made lightly, overseas, were easily overruled in Muslim culture? I have a pen pal, in Iran. She got married. (I wrote many fewer letters, for obvious reasons). She had a kid. Her husband beat the crap out of her. She had to divorce him; she said she was afraid she'd lose her eyesight, he was beating her so badly. She lost custody of her kid, as do most Muslim women getting a divorce. She was shamed by divorce. She unloaded some of what she felt, in letters. I did the small things I could, to put some light in her life. For a time, I was the one kind voice in her world.

But just like moths seek out light, the eternal dance of polarity continues. So, maybe you want a kid. Maybe you tell the guy you're on the pill, and he doesn't need the condom. And you "forget" to take the pill.

Many women feel it's ok to make a kid, without having a man around to help raise the kid[58]. OK. Here is why your son needs a man around. Yeah, you can raise him by yourself, and it's been done. He still needs a Sensei, who has been down the path he's on.

When he's crazy with lust, and hormones, at 17, he needs to hear a man talking quietly about why one always uses a condom, at least; how pregnancy totally changes the girl's life, about how it's better not to risk getting a girl pregnant, about how to avoid women on the prowl, how child support works, and so on.

He will copy the men he sees[59]. If you have a new boyfriend in, every month [not so uncommon now], he learns something about commitment, in relationships. I've been around men who grew up without fathers. They are generally bitter about it.

Your daughter? Does she need a father around? Well, female children of single mothers are more promiscuous[60]. They tend to marry older men, or very inappropriate men, to get that sort of daddy energy they didn't get when young. And if you complain about men being irresponsible, etc., guess what programming she is picking up?

---

58 P. 173, *Why Men Fear Marriage*, R.M. Johnson, New York: Simon and Schuster, 2009. I know a guy who was separated from his wife, who had just this to happen to him. The new amour told him if he went back to his wife, she would destroy him, economically. He did, and she is. Word of mouth advertising is incredibly effective; he shares the story often.

59 Some years ago, a woman was talking with admiring tones about how this female doctor had artificial insemination, to have a son. She was just in awe of how she didn't need a man. I pointed out that I knew several single mothers, including my sister at the time, and none of them were glad they didn't have a man around, especially with a son. I also pointed out that when he gets to be 9 or 10, he'll be asking where his dad is. The woman seemed to have some interest in me, or so my intuition said. But she had just explained she didn't need a man around. Why would I have anything to do with a woman like that? She was a gorgeous blonde, but she provided free intel about other problems. Threat Level Yellow. Stealth mode. Evade.

60 They missed out on being protected and cherished by a man, and so get bad boys, who treat them badly. P. 120, *Calling in "The One"*, Katherine Woodward Thomas, New York: Three Rivers Press, 2004.

People marry what is in their subconscious minds[61]. If you hate men, I guarantee you your daughter, and son, will pick up on it. Children don't do what we tell them, no, they imitate us. They copy what we do. They absorb our programming.

Two mature parents do a better job than one. They form a soliton, a standing wave form, that gives out more energy than is put into it, because it is at a higher level of order. For a man, a good woman, in a committed relationship, is like plugging into power. For me, it's like meditating on the Chi, aka the Force, of the *Star Wars* movies.

Women get the same kind of benefit. I knew a couple like this, in a church I used to attend. Their energy was crackling. Both looked at least 10 years younger than their chronological age. Both were very, very happy. I've seen others, also.

And for every feminist who bitches about the patriarchy, and so on, I ask you, where did the chain start? Every man who is cruel was taught that, by having cruelty inflicted on him. But, as feminists believe, men feel no pain[62].

Every Don Juan using and dumping women had his heart broken. Violence, and kindness, are both gifts that keep on giving. Germaine Greer, and Gloria Steinem, both had quite a bit of trauma, when they were younger. They revenged themselves on men, very effectively.

What did Gloria say? A woman without a man is like a fish without a bicycle. I don't know of any man who wants to be a fish's bicycle. Threat Level Red. Cloak. Evade. Gloria did find her bicycle, though, didn't she. Her advice did at times sound fishy, to me.

---

61 P. 130 , *Calling in "The One"*, Katherine Woodward Thomas, New York: Three Rivers Press, 2004.

62 In Zaire, people choose to believe sorcerers feel no pain; Sorcerers, caught, are beat to a pulp. Feminists believe men feel no pain, for the same reason, so they can hurt them in every possible way, and feel no remorse. I have seen this myself. So have many smart men. Threat Level Red.

J. What will it be? Kindness or violence?

Revenge is a pitcher with a hole in it. No matter how much you pour in, it is never enough. And the violence gets passed on. Yes, you as a woman, can savage a man, and cut him up. The next woman to get him has to clean up after you. Is that the legacy you want to leave behind? And what better way to reinforce the sisterhood, than to leave a huge mess for the next woman to clean up. Or not clean up, because the man won't get involved with her... and she can complain that the only men available are slackers.

Adults know that actions have consequences, right, Dr. Sax? Isn't that part of being an adult? Which is more useful, kindness, or violence?

Over thirty years ago, a woman was kind to me, at a time when I greatly needed it. I have no idea why. She had every reason not to do so. Other than my parents, she was my most important teacher. I knew I would never have a relationship with her, of course, even then.

If I saw that woman today, I would place my knees on the ground, and bow my head to the ground, for her, the way I saw Orientals do for high level Buddhist spiritual masters, when I was a kid. I would cry my eyes out. I would thank her from the depths of my being. But I won't ever see her again.

I have passed on her kindness to me, paying it forward, ten thousandfold. I am called El Reverendo, in the city near where I live, in the Hispanic community, because that is the only way they could understand the charity I do.

It is extremely difficult to take the violence inflicted on one, and to break the chain- to not pass it on. It takes great strength. I do so based on what I've learned, particularly from her example.

What do you want to pass on? Kindness, or violence? The feminists have made their choice, and it's obvious. This is why most men avoid them like the plague. Yes, you can find exceptions.

Kindness, or violence? Which will it be, today?

Relationships with the opposite gender are a direct reflection of intent. Intent is a symptom of a belief system. It's not the trauma that hurts us- it is our INTERPRETATION of it, the belief system we create, that hurts us.

I was very hurt by girls, when I was younger. I was so hurt, I didn't even see or hear the girls who later approached me, politely, seeking relationship with me. I could have kicked myself, in the debriefs I did for myself, later... but I learned from my mistakes.

Nick Hockings, an Ojibwa elder, told me that dance is the heart of the culture. He couldn't understand why Anglo men didn't dance. I do. When I was 11, I was in a place that had square dancing. I asked a girl to go, beforehand. She said no. I went stag. Several other girls weren't interested.

OK, I said, and I never danced again, till I was in college. I happily worked during the nights my high school held the proms.

I know, now, that there were at least 20 nice lasses in my high school class, that would have been happy to go with me. I wasn't about to give them a chance [to hurt me], though. What fool dreamed that torture up? Indigenous cultures have circle dance, as at Dances of Universal Peace.org or whatever their website is. Everyone has a place. This is a healthy model.

There is a woman who teaches flirting, Susan Rabin. I went to her course. She said women had to learn to face rejection, just like men do. Uhh, yes. It's not so easy to put yourself on the line, is it, women[63]?

K. Another secret that women don't know about men

That's all very well. Now I will say some things I've never seen in print. When my father was dating, in the 1950's, one woman he was with broke it up, telling him she was lesbian.

---

63 Remember those guys in high school that women cut, deep to the heart, with contemptuous rejection? Did you really think that energy wouldn't go anywhere? Now those guys have a field of women to choose from, which just gets better, as they get older. Even eye candy women have trouble finding mates, beyond 30 or so, I've noticed...

He commented she went on to marry another guy, and have children. A dispassionate observer would realize she wasn't lesbian. She was smart enough to let him down easy. He had used this trick himself.

Sauce for the goose is sauce for the gander, don't you think? I remember going out with a woman, a divorcee. She was nice enough. But I found things out from her. She was a died in the wool feminist. I did what I could, to help her heal from her ex. At some point, my intuition, my guardian angel- whatever name you like- told me she was not the one. It told me I had graduated from her school, already.

My father told me a man can never break off a relationship, you have to let the woman do it, or she has no closure. She has to believe she has the power, in the relationship. My father shared many proverbs, which are the concentrated wisdom of the whispers of my ancestors. Here's one that applies: *Hell hath no fury like that of a woman scorned*[64].

So, I let my intent flow, and I started effortlessly acting like a slacker, or a jerk. A polite jerk, but a jerk. It was an effortless role to get into. And she broke it off. Why would I want to give her a complex? I don't. Leaving a jerk is easy. There is no shame in leaving a jerk. No reason to pig out on chocolates, Ben and Jerry's ice cream, and donuts. The woman can talk about how all men are jerks, with her girlfriends, and they will agree with her, reinforcing her in this comfortable belief system, that lets them feel superior to men. She knows she's still the Princess.

Later, she wanted to get back together again, but I just never responded to her letter. Once in role, stay in role.

I've never seen any of this in print, ever, anywhere. It wouldn't matter, women don't listen to men, usually. Unlike, perhaps, some men, I listen when women talk. Intently. I've had enough pain in my life, from not paying attention to my environment, that I take it all in. I debriefed every mistake, and calibrated what I needed, intuitively, to avoid making it again.

---

64 Consider the movie portrayal of this, in *Fatal Attraction*, and *Vanilla Sky*, which, by way, is better in its original Spanish version, *Abre los Ojos*. I've seen rejected women do some crazy things.

I remember overhearing an extensive discussion from a woman, who talked about trying to get a man, and how hard it was, and how the men wouldn't call her after the first date. She got her hair done, got clothes, etc., but couldn't seem to get past the first date. She was unloading to her female friends. It sounded agonizing.

She described the men as being very cruel. She sounded like she had quite a bit of resentment in her, also. When I pick up resentment, intuitively, it feels like burning embers on my skin. With her, it felt like I had a flamethrower on me.

As she was finishing up, maybe 30 minutes later (it was during a break in a seminar, I had nothing else to do), I chanced to look at her. I understood immediately what the problem was. She had a hairstyle which made her look a good 15 years older, if not like granny.

She had major carbohydrate toxicity, in the form of being a good 50 pounds over her ideal weight. Pancake makeup didn't conceal blemishes on her face, which told me the sewage system was backing up. Sexual attraction matters. And being pleasant is far, far more important.

Is a man going to risk his financial future, in a grand throw of the dice, on an angry whale? She reminded me of the Mimi character, on that old Drew Carey TV show. Threat Level Red. Stealth Mode. Evade[65].

One of my aunts had a friend, a woman, who took off over 600 pounds, with Weight Watchers. She got the highest award they give. She was so overweight that she went to the bathroom once, and gave birth. She had no idea she was pregnant. The grown up child was on the police force in town. Yes, she was married. Her husband liked her cooking. More importantly, she was very pleasant. Note that. Her husband could put up with the weight, because <u>SHE WAS PLEASANT</u>[66].

---

65 I did not offer any advice. Women this irritated will hurt the messenger.
66 I forget what book I read, where they asked what men most wanted, in a wife. The majority answer was "turn off the bitching gene, and turn up the sex to high." Women seem to do the opposite, and then wonder why their relationships with men aren't going well. Women don't listen.

If you had a dog, and you whipped it regularly every day, to get it to do what you wanted, how does the dog react? It starts hiding, it starts running away and not coming back when you call, in time it completely avoids you. Isn't that right? Otherwise, you eventually break its spirit[67]. So why do women think that bitching and fuming is going to get them what they want, from a man?

Doesn't a man deserve at least the treatment a beloved dog would get? So many women haven't figured this out. How do you feel when you hear a little kid whining? That's what bitching sounds like, to a man.

Maybe men aren't exactly what they appear to be? Maybe they know a little more about evading? Maybe, as they get smarter, they avoid bad deals? Any used car salesman can tell you what a great deal you're getting, on the lot. Do you trust, or believe them? Is it really much different in relationships?

L. Men have a breaking point, in relationships

Sometimes it is reached on the first date, or even before. Women don't seem to realize this. I know a Native American craftsman. He is a simple guy, he makes his living with his hands. His eyes are incredibly deep. He has no masks, talking with him is like talking to his deep self, his soul.

His wife of over 20 years decided to run off with an Italian[68] guy. He took over caring for their four children.

---

67 If this talk about men being intuitive bothers you, you can talk to your female friends, and they'll assure you it's a fantasy. Your male friends will also assure you it's fantasy, and you can go back to your comfortable existence, knowing that the available men are slacker man-boys, that you can comfortably and quite correctly feel superior to.

68 There is an Italian count, Lequio, who lives in Spain. He makes his living from appearing in the gossip press, now. He is a gifted seducer. His mentress was a Spanish woman, a master of the gossip press. He had a kid with her, and dumped her. One of the women he seduced was the daughter of a very powerful man. Of course Lequio planned to dump her, also. One night, some men with no necks showed up at his house. They had a lengthy discussion on the high cost of dental repair work, healing rates for broken bones in casts, the difficulty of making a living while also dealing with severe blunt trauma to the head, and that sort of thing, which ended up with him being thrown into a dumpster. At a subsequent press conference, he noted that the woman was the love of his life, and he had every intention of spending the rest of his life with her. These were called "come to Jesus" meetings, when I was a kid. I was truly touched by his newfound commitment to traditional marriage, and his new wife. I found it inspiring. Yes, fidelity is a fine thing. His first wife can't speak of him without cursing, though.

She came back, about a year and a half later, wanting to make it as it was. He said no. He told her she had written a letter, saying goodbye to her children, and that he and the children couldn't ever trust her again. He had custody, and title to the house.

Why leave a strong position, for a weak position with someone who can't be trusted? I guess that story won't make it into *Chicken Soup for the Soul.* Women don't realize that men have a breaking point. Once it is passed, it is passed.

I went to a marriage counselor, with my second wife. He asked a very intelligent question: "Do you both of you want to make this work?" I tried to say yes. But months of being screamed at by a drunk, rabid, bitchy, lying banshee came out of me, all of a sudden, as a soul-rooted NOOOOOOOOOOOOOOOOOOOOOOOOOOOOOOOOOOOOOOOOOO!

Dr. Laura Schlessinger[69] notes women seem totally unaware that men have a breaking point. I had reached mine. For women, relationships are like the control board of a nuclear power plant, I mean, it's that complex for them.

For men, it's an on-off switch. Do you remember the movie *Meet the Parents*, where the Robert DeNiro character talks about being inside, or outside, the circle of trust? That is exactly how it works, for a man[70].

At critical mass, of harassment, the on switch gets turned off, and the woman exits the zone of trust. Few men will marry a woman who is outside of their circle of trust, and they need some serious denial to do so. The older a man gets, the more it takes to turn the switch on, to open up that zone of trust. I talk to older men, who play the personals. They have no problem cold-calling lots and lots of women, before they find one they are comfortable with. They know the serious pain of just "settling", instead of selecting.

---

69 Hate her as you wish, she sometimes has relevant ideas. I'll take my awareness any way I can get it. Feminist literature reads like the *Volkischer Beobachter,* with a new target, to me, but I read it anyway, to learn. Awareness beckons to us all the time. I know the words feminists use, so I can quarantine them quickly, before they can do damage to me. Men really do adapt.

70 If you read Barbara De Angelis' books on relationships, and even R.M. Johnson's book, *Why Mean Fear Marriage*, getting into a committed relationship with a man involves gently entering that zone of trust, until you live there. R.M. Johnson has ten tips for that, in his book, and Barbara has even more.

I take spiritual seminars, as often as I can. They are 80%+ attended by women. Sometimes there will be exercises where people talk. I listen. I am amazed by the number of women over 25 who just know they have a soulmate. Some are rather overweight.

If I was single, and knew I had a soulmate with the intensity that these women do, I would be doing everything I could to improve myself, in every way, to make a good first impression, if nothing else. Even the book *The Secret* says to do this.

Are they? Almost uniformly, no. They aren't. I spoke with one woman who had at least 40 extra pounds on. An intuitive had told her she had a soulmate coming, a military guy. Her attitude was that he would just love her as she was. OK, but that's not a roulette wheel I would want to play. Military guys are somewhat more sensitive to weight issues, too.

They all think the guy will love them just as they are. Cool. And with all that extra weight, and acidic body pH, will they have the energy to deal with the stress of family? Uhh, probably not.

And if they are overweight, AND unpleasant... this is like my father's generation seeing a cord around a field, with flags that say *Achtung! Minen!*[71] That soulmate may show up. But minefields are known to be hazardous to one's health. The switch can be turned off, at first contact.

What is the quick way out, the default solution, the automatic eject button? Just be a slacker, a jerk. The transition may not even be conscious. Have you ever dealt with people, and it felt like you were playing a part in their life, that they wrote the script for?

M. Women teach many lessons, to the aware

I don't go to gentleman's clubs, or stripper joints. I can't stand being in bars, or places that serve alcohol. I have found these not useful, for me. I'd rather get people talking, and learn. Women have many useful lessons to teach, for those open to learning.

---

71 German for "*Heads up! Mines!*" an indication of a mine field, full of explosive mines that will blow up if stepped on. That's what dealing with bitchy women feels like, for a man.

The lesson of extra weight is usually that their body is putting that fat around severe unresolved trauma, and toxin load, like an oyster puts pearl around a grain of sand. I was married to a woman with a lot of pain. Her painkiller was alcohol.

I told her once it felt like she was taking out all the hurt men had ever given her, on me. She said, "Yep, that's right." I value clarity in communication. Women like this are a ticking time bomb, even if they have their own house, and great career. My name is not Jesus, and I don't like paying for other people's sins. Few people do.

Another thing women taught me was to <u>never</u> rescue them. They will never forgive a man who does that. You see, when you play the victim, that means you have to have a persecutor. I married not one, but two women, who played this game. I foolishly rescued them. But you can't play the game of being a victim without a persecutor, so they turned me into their persecutor[72].

I saw my first wife for the first time on a summer day, when I was in college. She was wearing white slacks, and an orange blouse. Oh, I was in love, and just didn't care. We got married. She really wanted a child, and we found a way to have one. It is much better to wait till you have a job, and so on, but we didn't think that way.

She just wanted to get away from her mother, and I was the convenient train West. She never was happy with me, after that first year. She was always complaining. Nothing was ever good enough. She turned me into her persecutor. She told me, before we got married, that she felt we would be married for five years, and then get divorced. I didn't listen. She was only off by three weeks[73].

That first wife found another rescuer- my best friend, and alcohol. She left our young daughter with me, which meant I got custody, and I went to court to do so. That was the only part of that relationship worth saving.

---

72 This is what it is like, for a man, to deal with a woman playing games: *They are playing a game. They are playing a game of not playing a game. If I show them I see the game, they will punish me. I must play their game of not seeing I see the game.*

73 [Chinese music. Visual of Shao Lin monastery. Cut to image of old Chinese dude, speaking.] "Grasshopper, you must learn to listen to your feelings. They will guide you. Learn to listen to women, also, because they will tell you what you need to know, about them."

She had five boyfriends that I knew about, after she had our child[74]. How did I know? She told me. She was that self-centered. Her new amour parroted her, and blamed me for what happened.

I saw him after three years, and I saw some serious pain in his eyes. He knew that he was riding the tiger, to use the Chinese expression, and couldn't get off. Suffering develops the soul. He clearly wanted a lot of soul development, and he was getting it.

She got pregnant shortly after shacking up with him, and she had three kids with him. Now, 25 years later, he is still paying for college, for the youngest. He can't live with his wife, either, due to her health problems. There is no justice, but there is balance. I bless them.

My decisions 32 years ago, that resulted in my beloved older daughter, had consequences. I was not able to get my dream job, because I chose to marry that woman. I love my daughter dearly, but I couldn't even think of applying for my dream job, as a single parent.

That daughter contacted me recently, asking if it was ok to give my contact info to her mother. I said absolutely not. She did nothing but cause me pain, and trouble, most of it unnecessarily. That switch will stay off. She will never again be in my circle of trust. She said herself that I was the nicest guy she knew, when we got married. I didn't have the slacker override program, then, though.

I rescued my second wife from a bad situation. She was an alcoholic[75]. She had some extremely unrealistic expectations. She wouldn't talk them out, she would just get angry when they weren't met, especially when I didn't know what they were.

---

74 Had I heard this before our child was conceived, I would have cut off anything that could produce babies, for 3 months, and then given her a one way bus ticket home, and said, "Gee, sorry it didn't work out, have a good life." Things are different when you have a kid.
75 She also didn't believe in doing housework. What housework got done was done by me, including cleaning up after her cat. She was constantly getting sick, and demanding to be taken care of. I learned a whole lot about taking nothing for granted, from my experience with her. She lied about everything, to "get the guy". She later told my mother she married me for my medical insurance, and paycheck. Didn't I feel special, then. And of course, she was a feminist, as I found out later. Her idea was that not only would I be the primary breadwinner, I would also do all the housework, and she would be sick, eating chocolates. My job was to amuse her. I told her once that she was very difficult to please. She said, with resentment, "You're a talented guy, you should appreciate the challenge!" Any desire to please her just drained out of me, like a liquid, then.

My personal favorite was to come home, and she'd be upset. I'd ask what was wrong. She would say, "If you loved me, you would know!" Now that is a logical bind. Gosh, I didn't know, which must mean I didn't love her, right? Just the thought to plant in a spouse's mind, for relationship maintenance...

She liked to scream at me, for lengthy periods. One of the things I do to relieve stress is to flex my hand, below my waist. I did so, once. She told my mother I had shaken my fist in her face. There is a legal term for this- assault. I have never shaken my fist in anyone's face, ever, in my life. If she had told a cop, or a judge this, what defense would I have? None. No cop, or judge, would believe me. She loved playing the victim.

The only defense from someone like her is absolute non-contact. I divorced her, as soon as I could. I haven't talked to her since. If she tried to talk to me, I would say, "On advice of counsel, I respectfully decline all communications with you." That switch is permanently off.

N. Sex has consequences

It feels great. The Chinese say it is the same force that shapes galaxies. It feels like heaven. Here's the kicker. If the guy gets her pregnant, he changes her life forever. It doesn't matter if she gets an abortion, or has the kid. It changes her life forever.

It changes his life, too. Sure, the man can run away. Those kids are like salmon, going to their home stream, though, they want to find their missing parents, for the rest of their lives. I don't want to do that to my kids. How do I prevent it? When I feel nervous, about a woman, I get the heck out of her space, ASAP, automatically, and semi-consciously.

One of my daughter's college boyfriends was about 30. He got an interesting phone call. It seemed a woman he was involved with, 10 years prior, had a child by him. She never told the boyfriend.

But the son started asking where his dad was, persistently enough that the woman tracked down the former boyfriend. Children given up for adoption are famous for tracking down their birth parents.

Better men, and women, who plan to bring children into the world, have enough respect for them to do so into a situation where they can raise them properly.

Accountants treat obligations that last 20 years as being about the same as lifetime obligations. How long does child support last? In my state, for the first child, the man owes 30% of pre-tax income, which is about half after tax income. How well can a man support a family, with half his income gone before he can touch it? Not very well. She can also take the man back to court, any time she feels like it, and get it increased. The man has no defense. Men hear this stuff.

The tennis player Boris Becker was with a woman, who offered to dispose of the condom after their did their thing. He found her in the bathroom, trying to insert its contents into her. I bet he was a little more careful about disposal, after that. As was every man who heard the story.

I have known at least twenty couples who had to get married, because the woman got pregnant. She went off birth control, but never bothered to tell her boyfriend that. That was her way of helping him along into commitment. Solidly placing oneself outside of the circle of trust, by using compulsion, is not the way to start a relationship...

My family has a family friend, what some might call a ridgerunner. She met a divorced guy she liked, at a bar. He was too slow to commit, for her. The guy lived with his mother. He was a hard worker, though, with a good job. One morning, our friend showed up at his mother's house, and told the guy's mother he was moving in with her. Mom had no objections, of course, and helped load the truck.

So when the guy got home that day, after work, his room was empty. He asked his mother what happened, and she told him he had moved. Now that is Sadie Hawkins in action. But she kept manipulating him, and otherwise irritating him. Some years later, they hate each other, and they are getting divorced.

My wife and I know of a guy in Spain, who helped a Filipina woman get her green card, or whatever they are in Spain, by marrying her.

They had an agreement, they'd be married only for whatever time she needed, and then she'd go. I have known Filipinos, they are remarkably intelligent, very grounded, and practical. And pleasant.

Here's a Filipina, already married, to a guy who works with computers. Why go looking elsewhere? She offered him some free stuff, she was "on the pill", but wasn't; he took the freebies, and she got pregnant.

But- BUT- she was smart enough to be very pleasant, and get into her Yin polarity, and irritate him as little as possible. He's very happy now, even though he knows he was manipulated. She was and is smart. Pigs get fat, hogs get slaughtered[76].

There are female high school graduates who get one way bus tickets to near Camp Lejeune, NC, and hook up with a lonely Marine, in a club, and stick him for child support. By way, a man under a child support order, who foolishly gets married to another woman, opens her income up to attachment, in addition to his.

That would really help the man's new relationship, wouldn't it? Especially since even getting a divorce won't stop the support order, once it exists, against the new wife's income, in some states. Some single mothers, with a kid, wonder why men aren't lining up to get exploited, in the same way[77]. Gosh, maybe it's because they've heard these stories?

O. Listen to people's stories

I like to get people talking, because I learn a lot that is not in books. I remember speaking with a Vietnam Veteran. He came back from the 'Nam, and married his high school sweetheart. Six weeks into the marriage, she said she wasn't happy. He said "who the heck is?" She told him she wanted out. He said ok, if that's what you want.

---

76 Filipina women, actually women in many countries, see unmarried men above about 25 as a sort of threat to society, unbalanced Yang. They go out of their way to fix up single guys, with a woman. They like balance. Americans... like fantasy.
77 My brother knows a guy, who got married to a woman with a child. She pressured him to adopt her child, legally. He did. Then she divorced him, and socked him with child support. How many men who heard that story will even go on a date with a single woman, who has a child, after hearing that story? Form a circle with your thumb, and forefinger.

Three months after the marriage, they were divorced. He was really broken up about it. His father told him to pay her the cash value of what they had in their house. This was good advice, for the time- the late 70's, as rising values covered his payout.

His ex went on to have a kid with hubby no. 2, who treated her badly, and then have another kid with hubby no. 3, who also mistreated her. Hubby No. 1 was looking very good, with these new comparables. Wisdom comes to all, eventually.

However, she had burned that bridge, torn out the foundations, and obliterated the approach road. The circle of trust was closed to her, now. Actions have consequences, and elements in systems adapt.

He also had no intention of paying to raise someone else's kids. He liked his ex's parents, though, and would sometimes have dinner with them. He would leave, afterwards, and thank them for the meal.

He told me he was at a wedding, and heard a young woman openly discussing her plan to marry three men, sequentially, have a child with each, and sock them all with child support and alimony. She said this quite openly. I know this will come as a shock to you, but the Vet wasn't the committing type, by then, this only confirmed his existing prejudices. He was a Don Juan. Don Juan is cold because his heart was broken.

He was getting a degree in accounting. He was dating what were called ADC women, at the time[78]. These were women receiving welfare payments, with children. They watched soap operas for much of the day. A Native American elder told me that your eyes eat images, the way your mouth eats food, and you become what you eat[79].

---

78 He got the idea because a 17 year old girl asked him to get her pregnant, with no intention of being married. He asked why. She said she wanted to go on welfare, and she needed a child to do this. If that's not a perverse incentive, what is? They made no attempt to determine paternity, at that time. He looked into it, and realized the possibilities. He decided that paternity would be tracked down, eventually, though, so he avoided fathering kids.

79 I've said this more than once. Are you careful what you feed your eyes, yet? I remember a couple who lived next door, many years ago. They loved to watch horror movies. Their son was a horror, who bothered other kids in the area, hitting them, and acting out what he way in movies. They never made the connection.

The ADC model of the world, he said, was that they were the queen bitch, with 3-4 men anxious to marry them, and they were playing the bitch[80], holding them off, for the heck of it[81], to play with their heads. Many TV shows, and movies, are about wishful thinking played out on screen[82].

He was with ADC women, and he got what he wanted from them. At that time, he kept about two on the line. Every now and then, one would try to corner him into commitment, he'd say something, and later decide it just wasn't going to work out. He put on the role of a slacker, a jerk, and let them get rid of him.

The men the ADC women were dating weren't as stupid as men in their early 20's. He said that when the women got to be about 35, and realized they could only get a man for the weekend, but not for marriage, they tended to get bitter, but that they were easily replaced. He didn't have to say much, they had a complete sequence of events, for him, already planned.

Let's take a systems view, here, and start looking at the chain.

---

80 I've actually seen books designed to teach women how to bring out the inner bitch. Let's discuss how useful this is. Would you say that the SS guards that ran Nazi concentration camps were some nasty people? I would. They were specifically trained to bring out the "inner schweinhund", the inner pighound- the male equivalent of the bitch. American women are bitchy as is, without special training. And these women want to DEVELOP this skill? One of those books, on a woman's bookshelf, is an automatic Threat Level Red, Danger Will Robinson, Stat, Incoming! Hit the dirt! message for me. It is a time to be very sick, to realize I'm actually gay, to go beyond merely being a slacker. Well, I'm married now, so I don't have to deal with this.

81 Spanish telenovela soap operas are totally different. In these, the virtous woman goes through hell, finally finds the prince, and the telenovela ends with the wedding. The bitches are called "malas" [evil women], in the telenovelas, and they are villainesses, who always get punished or end up badly, usually in the last week of the telenovela. In American soaps, the bitches are the heroines, and always win. Think very carefully about the fundamental difference between Hispanic and English culture, here, and how the malas are the heroines for American women who watch soap operas. When Don Francisco's *Sabado Gigante* TV show runs video of Anglo men who have Hispanic wives or girlfriends, and are clearly very, very happy, the audience is amused. Hispanic women usually know when they have it good, with a man, and appreciate it. Anglo women tend to complain, a lot, no matter how good they have it. Their standards are very different. This is directly due to the images in their minds. Smarter men know to find out what images a woman has in her mind, long before they commit. I mentioned to a Hispanic woman I know only through the Internet that I was engaged to a Hispanic woman. That first woman, who knew me only via email, sent me books of Spanish love poetry at her own expense, Priority Mail, and noted that I was getting a very special woman. Relationships are handled differently, in Latin culture.

82 My mother used to love the TV program *Murder She Wrote*, for example, because the smart older female protagonist sets all the idiot men straight. I used to love *MacGyver.*

His one high school sweetheart, by dumping him, and taking him for what she could get, passed on how much heartbreak, to how many women, for how many years... not exactly the path of Mother Theresa, huh?

He said the ADC ladies had an extraordinarily unrealistic view of life. Once, he got up late, and had to call in, to work, to say he was going to be late. He couldn't understand why the alarm clock didn't work. His girlfriend of the time said he looked so peaceful, sleeping, she turned it off. After that, he had a wristwatch alarm.

Often, when he said he had to go to work, his girlfriends would say, "Just take the day off", the way the male stars of soap operas do. They got regular cost of living increases, free movie tickets, and many other things working folks don't get. He said they had totally unrealistic ideas about money. No surprise- they were married to the state.

He said he'd never marry one. The maintenance costs were just too high. Another reason for this was that he didn't want to pay to raise somebody else's kids. He said if he had to pay to raise a dog, he wanted to name it, train it, and so on. Interesting analogy.

P. The simple solution: default, or least energy path

He was very lucky he didn't have a child with the first wife, of course. Explaining to a child why mommy and daddy will be living in separate places is painful. I watched my first daughter cry her eyes out for a month, when her mom left. The default solution? Don't have kids. I have known a number of married men who don't want children, because they see them as financial destruction bombs just waiting to go off.

I remember a First Sergeant, in the Army. He found out his wife was playing around. So he played around, but didn't divorce her right away. She sued for divorce. The judge said he'd "forgiven" her, so her adultery didn't count. His did. He had to move out of the house, and pay her all but $100/month of his income. That's right, he was expected to live on $100/month.

If you can get most men over 30 talking, you will hear stories like this. If. Most men will not tell women stories like this, for obvious reasons, and even I wrote this book under a pseudonym. These stories are very much part of their measure of situations with women.

I knew a guy in the Army, who had 3 girlfriends at all times. If one left, she was replaced right away. None knew of the others. I have enough trouble with one, I can't imagine the logistical arrangements for three.

You might suspect some trauma, some emotional scar tissue, behind this behavior, and you'd be right. He had some incredible charm, with the ladies, most of which involved letting them project their fantasies onto him. He had no intention of having children, or getting married, ever.

I know a guy, who is 40. He makes over $100K a year, and owns his own house. He can get people laughing any time. He won't get serious with a woman. He doesn't trust women, based solely on the experience of his friends, not even his own. Women don't seem to understand that when they use scorched earth tactics on a man, the next woman to get him pays the price, and the next woman to get the guy who heard the story pays the price, too.

Many single women are looking for their fantasy soulmate, and seem totally oblivious to what goes on in life, for men, with relationships[83]. Women in college, sometimes even up to the age of 30, set extremely high standards for what they want, in a man[84]. Many don't find it. Their standards start dropping, around 27, or so.

---

83 Some men I know would willingly walk away from a soulmate even if they knew she was a soulmate, given their life experience with women. Oh, wait, that doesn't fit the model, does it? No, it doesn't. That doesn't make it any less real. And many men don't recognize their soulmates, or so at least forty women have told me. Some men aren't open to the intuitive communications that would let them know this. So, maybe improving oneself in advance could be a good idea...

84 They want a guy who starts at a six figure income, with at least a Lexus, who can and will take time off from work any time to pay attention to her, who has a staff of servants to keep up the house, who gives her a credit card with a five figure credit limit, and acts generally like the male stars of soap operas. I'm not kidding, this is real. Listen to women complaining to each other, you'll get an incredible education. Women in their 20's have an ideal picture of a man, and house, and complain mercilessly about any gap between reality and that comparable image. Your education would broaden if you could watch morning soap operas, on TV, one day. This is a reflection of how many American women see the world. No man can match the fantasy men of soap operas, or Romance novels, any more than any woman can match the plastic ladies of *Playboy* magazine. *Playboy's* models can't even match the centerfolds. It's all Photoshop.

A demographic shift occurs, around the age of 27, or so. The number of available men dries up. They are married, slackers, or otherwise unavailable. I saw many men in the military, who wanted nothing to do with women. They had been hurt too much by women. They weren't gay, they just weren't interested in women. They had become the warrior monks the military prefers.

My mother would say that they were going to the wrong bars, and my grandmother would say that they should have sought wives in church, not in bars. Their trauma is real enough, though, and they don't have the experience to know that.

I was told by many men that the clubs around military posts, an area where the demographic male/female ratio is high, always had more women than men. My housemate, who regularly trolled clubs, told me himself he was ugly, and he never had trouble finding a woman he liked, for the night[85].

I never saw him lacking for ladies, on weekends. He had married women making appointments to see him- I saw it with my own eyes. I would never take a risk like that myself. He told me he didn't even have to tell them he loved them. He was twice divorced, and wasn't about to go further than a night or two.

Don Juan can do what he does because of the scar tissue on his broken heart. Have you noticed that a woman who refuses relationships is respected, as independent and liberated? A man who refuses relationships is afraid of commitment. Yes, Virginia, there really is a double standard[86].

---

85 I never trolled the clubs. Weekends were time spent with my child, who needed attention.

86 The commander of the *Exxon Valdez,* an oil tanker involved in a major oil spill, was really exhausted, but ordered to pilot the ship anyway. He didn't actually kill anybody. He was crucified in the press, and lost his job. About the same time, a female FAA controller guided a plane into the ground, killing all passengers aboard. She was put into grief counseling, given time off, and generally treated very well. Her name wasn't even released to the press. The grinding disrespect shown men, since the early 1970's, in the media, in the U.S., just doesn't help. My father told me that when he was young, it really meant something to be a father. People had a lot of respect for fathers, and mothers, much more so than today. My wife expresses it in the same way. To be male, in Spain, means you show up to work, take care of your family, pay your bills, and get the job done. Macho simply means male, in Spain, it has none of the connotations it has in English. Nowadays, in the U.S., it is perfectly alright for a man to father children, and walk away from them. It is weird to see government agencies promoting fatherhood, now, because they finally understand that not having fathers around causes serious problems. Men, particularly minority

I remember a joke I heard, about this demographic shift. Why won't a man under 35 commit? Lack of experience. Why won't a man over 35 commit? Experience. There's nothing quite like carving up a man in divorce court, and hanging him up from a steer hook, to bleed out, to scare other men.

Any man over 30 has seen at least one friend through the divorslaughterhouse, in this way. These men know that when a man is in divorce court, he's already in the wrong, the only question is how much it is going to cost him, and how long he will get to bleed out.

There is only one way to deal with the Office of the Holy Inquisition, with any hope of success. That is arranging your life so you never have to deal with the grand inquisitor. What is the default, least energy path way to do that? Stay out of the mantrap, and don't commit.

A woman in her early 40's, who had her own house, a great career, and a daughter from a previous marriage, asked me, some years ago, why her boyfriend didn't want to tie the knot, and have children. She really, really wanted more children. She sought an honest answer. I gave her one.

I explained to her that for a man over 30, marriage, and especially children, appear to be a sword of Damocles[87], a ticking time bomb of economic devastation for life, controlled by an emotionally unstable being with capricious moods[88], full of resentments, who wouldn't appreciate good treatment but would always demand more, who might even be a Lesbian looking for child support[89].

---

men, are marginalized in many parts of society, and they have less and less trust of others.

87 Whoops, more old Greek stories. Damocles really envied a rich man. The rich man invited him to a great dinner. Damocles was really enjoying it. He chanced to look up. He saw a sword, hanging by a thread, such that the thread could break at any time, and the sword would fall, and hurt him greatly. He asked the rich man what that was about. The rich man said you envied me so much, I wanted you to understand what my life was like. That is exactly what it feels like, to be married to most American women, for a man over 30.

88 I knew a guy in college, who told me his mother was mentally unstable, and would regularly awaken his father, to beat him with her fists. His father could do... nothing. Now there's a word of mouth advertisement for marriage, don't you think? Feminists would tell him it was all his imagination, since women don't abuse men.

89 I heard of a guy in the Air Force, whose wife got him to take out a mortgage to build their dream home. When it was finished, she got a divorce. She got the house, and moved into it with her Lesbian lover. Guess who had to pay for it? Word of mouth advertising is the most effective kind. I heard that story in 1987, and look how long it has lasted, already. I've seen similar cases.

I explained to her, further, that if the woman has a daughter, from another marriage (she did), the man knows that if this capricious, moody teenager tells him she wants $100 cash, now, or she calls the police to allege molestation, he is down for the count. He has no defense, no matter what happened[90].

If she has a teenage boy, what happens when that kid drops the man's watch in the toilet, and says, "What are you going to do about it?" The only safe answer, and the one that keeps the man out of jail, is "Leave your mother today". Or better yet, use the least energy path, and never get involved with a woman who has children, in the first place[91].

I have a friend in NY City, who bought a condo with his girlfriend. They can't sell it. The girlfriend's son is stealing his possessions, and also storing illegal drugs in the condo, to sell. The mother is in total denial. He locks the door to the room he sleeps in.

Why tell you all this? This is the real world. I divorced two alcoholic women. I have since remarried, to a Hispanic woman. They usually still understand respect for their husbands[92]. I am happy with my wife, contento con mi esposa. Hablo la idioma para mi esposa.

I like intelligence in a woman, but not if there's any chance it will be used against me, and two-faced people scare me. Rattlesnakes are beautiful, too, but that doesn't mean I want to live with one. I've been cured.

No doubt it goes the other way, also, but women are far more willing to talk about their pain, and experience, than men are. Men are so used to male-bashing, they hear it so often, so they just walk away, silently[93].

Somehow, women think men don't pay attention.

90 I heard a story tonight. A family gave temporary shelter to a teenage girl, who had nowhere to go. She started making up tales about molestation. She was asked to leave, immediately. This is the least energy path solution.

91 I am aware that there are some very nice single women who have children. Men are aware of this pattern, however. The race does not always go to the swift horse, but that is the way to cast your bets. That is the least energy path.

92 Eastern European, Asian, Latin, and even African women are told by their mothers, as teens, that they aren't the Princess, and that if they can find a man who works, brings home the money, stays sober most of the time, treats them well, and does things for the kids, that they need to appreciate what they have. American women seem, often, to have been taught that they should always demand more, and never appreciate what they have. What's wrong with this picture?

93 Look at the male-bashing in *Brave*, Pixar's recent release. If they had bashed blacks, or

This is one reason men participate less and less in social functions... and in committed relationships with women.

My nephew's friend decided to join the U.S. Marine Corps. I shared with him some of what you read here. My sister hated it, she said I should have been telling him men were bad, that I was saying all women were bad. Not at all.

What I was doing was sharing some practical awareness, in the limited time I had to speak with him. I have said the same thing to several young men. They thank me, later, for having told them what I said, because it proved accurate. They also tell me that other men said the same kind of thing, to them.

Feminists[94] are the worst of the lot. I wear the largest wedding ring I could find. I still get hit on, especially by feminists. Even in the presence of my wife. I don't need to have anything to do with women so desperate they hit on married men. There is no justice, but there is balance. I can look at them just like the girls looked at me, in high school.

Well, I don't, I put on the totally unaware act, which is so much more fun. Let them tell their girlfriends about the clueless guy...

I hear language nowadays, about deconstructing sexist gender roles. It's really funny. The traditional roles lasted a long time, because they were stable. Demographics is the future. How many children does the average feminist have? Oh wait, motherhood is bad, for them. Maybe one, if that. Whatever they are deconstructing, it seems they will vanish like the Shakers.

How many children does the average Muslim, or Mormon, couple have? Uh huh. They aren't deconstructing traditional roles, are they? Is feminism sustainable, over generations? They are deconstructing something, but it's not what they think.

---

women, that way, it wouldn't have survived two weeks.

94 This should not be construed to say that I disrespect feminists. Quite the reverse. I have the same extreme, totally attentive, wary respect for them that I would for a Russell's Viper. I don't hate them, either. I just stay away from them, as I would from a Russell's Viper, or any other venomous critter. Yellow Jackets, and feminists, taught me lessons I never forgot.

I use the analogy of the patrol. There are some things my wife knows more about than I do. Then she is the patrol leader, and I follow her lead. There are things I know more about. If I need to offer ideas, to support where I want to go, I do so. For matters that don't really matter, I also defer to her. I have no problem asking for directions, either. Directions are useful. The point man keeps the patrol out of ambushes, also.

Q. Polarity is real

Benjamin Disraeli married a woman with white hair, and told her quite openly it was for her money. She just smiled. She had a quiet, low stress, relaxed home for him to come home to. She didn't bitch, complain, or scold, she just got him talking, and drained out his stress.

It wasn't long before he told her that if he'd known what he was getting into, he'd have married her for love. What did she do? She went into her Yin polarity. This, for a woman, is plugging into power. Both genders spend time in both polarities. Life is ebb and flow.

About 90% of prison inmates are men, while about 10% are women. About 90% of psychiatric clients are women. Few men go to shrinks. There is a Spanish joke, that after the divorce, the women goes to her therapist, and the man goes to his [new] girlfriend.

Yin is usually called the female polarity. Yang is the male. Men are never pure Yang, however, and women are never pure Yin. Every person is always a mix. You can ask a lesbian couple who the dominant one is, and they'll tell you they share everything. Uh huh. BS. Put two people together, and the one with more Yang dominates. Period.

They may play games, but they do. My wife has a relative, who is built like a linebacker. She got married to a very small man, in macho Francoist Spain. She dominated the marriage, and he died, young. Yang is yang, wherever it shows up.

My sister's husband dumped her, when she had young kids. She has said he was her greatest teacher. She learned to be a lot more Yang, with him, starting with the divorce court. He expected her to live on

$500/month. I would have said it's cheaper to keep her, but I wasn't asked. To raise her kids, she had to shift her Yin/Yang balance. One does what one must, in life.

Get a woman really, really mad, so her Yang dominates, and anger keeps her from considering consequences of her actions. You'll stay out of her way. She can hurt you. I used to know a woman who might have weighed 90 lbs soaking wet. She would face down drug dealers armed with automatic weapons[95], and make them go away. The only weapons are what is between your ears, and under your mastoid process.

I pay attention to the energy flow of all relationships. A woman who has more Yang, who dominates, at times, may be useful, if the man is going to travel, for work, and she will raise children. Women rule the house, generally, whether from the Yin or Yang.

If she is violent, the man knows he will have a most unpleasant life. Yes, violent women exist. The mass media is all lies, and they ignore much of what really goes on.

Look at Madonna. She had a kid with her personal trainer. I wonder if she even lets him see his kid? She married Guy Ritchie, who is about ten years younger. That broke up[96]. She plays with boytoys, now. A man knows he can marry a woman much richer than he is, who has her own house, and great career. What is he, to her? She is Barbie, with the house, the clothes, the car, and now she has that other accessory, Ken, with him. Now there's a recipe for self-esteem.

You heard about how much Divorced Barbie costs, right? That's because she comes with Ken's house, car, other possessions.... Men don't laugh at that joke. It's like a rape joke, it just isn't funny. Then there's the other side. Stedman Graham never did marry Oprah, did he? I wonder why.

---

95 Typically Uzis. Now this is interesting, as it is not legal to own them. Where are all those automatic Uzis coming from? Miami is flooded with them, for example. Here's a hint: They weren't stolen, they were not imported legally, and there is no legal way to acquire them. In fact there is no law that can stop their acquisition. This will help you realize how much crap there is, in the media. Over 80% of firearms deaths are due to the drug trade. Terence McKenna pointed out 30 years ago that the illegal drug trade is run by governments, as a way to raise money. Oh, forget I said that.

96 He apparently did to her what many women do to rich men. There is no justice, only balance.

Could it be that, even as Wikipedia says, that despite his other accomplishments, he is mainly known as Oprah's guy? What does that do for his self-image, I wonder? To be Ken?

I remember seeing the late night comedians' jokes about Ashton Kutcher, with Demi Moore. I wonder if that affected his decision to end their relationship? In more traditional cultures, women tend to marry men who are 5-10 years older, because the men have settled down. This used to be true in Europe, and Russia, particularly.

Men, generally, put about 90% of their attention on work, and 10% on relationships. Unless the men are slackers[97]. For women, generally, it is the reverse.

Men with any brains at all know that relationships are a lot of work. They know they have to start with great material. Did Michelangelo start with crummy, cracked marble? No, he got the best stuff he could get, from Carrera. He was done with his statues after at most two years, right? A man who is committed knows the marriage is forever, because the financial commitment might as well be forever.

Why would he start with anything less than the best he can get? A woman who has no understanding of polarity, respect, diet, duty, or anything beyond her own desires- what kind of marble is she? To play with the quantum mechanics metaphor, she isn't marble. She is wood. Wood gets burned. Or ignored. Or evaded.

R. Poisonous snakes are not good pets

A man with brains knows better than to keep poisonous snakes as pets. I choose not to drink alcohol. I sometimes go to *Alcoholics Anonymous* meetings, even so, and just listen. Especially to the female alcoholics.

I want my senses carefully calibrated, to the point where I can pick them out at 50 yards, so I can stay away from them. My brother is actually much better at this than I am.

---

97 Tim Allen did a great riff on this. Women have so many choices- marry, not marry, children, no children, work, no work. Men have two choices: work, or the penitentiary, basically. Slackers are just putting off these choices.

He used to be able to look at someone, at 30 yards, on the street, and tell me what drugs they were using.

I've learned that common sense isn't so common. If you were black, would you date someone in the Triple K? Well you could, and it's not like it's never happened, however, it would probably be unwise, don't you think? I mean, like, that would be stupid, right?

Can we agree that it would be unwise to date a person who has residual, visceral hatred of people like you? It would be kind of like keeping explosive ordnance in your apartment, that could go off at any time, or lighting cigarettes with open containers of gasoline nearby, or playing with poisonous snakes.

There is a group, in our society, that has, usually, a lot of residual hatred for men. They are sometimes called Feminists. Oh, they'll assure you they are just interested in women's rights, as surely as the Triple K folks are only interested in rights for white people[98].

I have heard both, and they sound to me like they are reading off the same script, with differences in the targets of their hatred, of course. I have read the literature of both groups. I will say the feminist stuff is somewhat more erudite, and less crude. The basic message is the same, though. Don't believe me, read their stuff.

I avoid both, with all the stealth I can muster. I don't do denial, any more. In the real world, denial has other names: insanity, and dysfunction. Denial is not useful, usually[99].

Relationships can be heaven- when polarity is in balance. Then you have current, or energy flow, and an electric relationship. Whatever you think about traditional roles, they were stable, like the lowest energy state of an electron.

---

98 They'll say that feminists have the radical notion that women are human beings. Hmm. I've never questioned that. They don't tell you the second half- and that men are not human beings. They believe this- one has but to listen to them talk.

99 Cristina Saralegui is the Hispanic Oprah, with over 100 million in her TV audience. About 1960, her father heard Fidel Castro, and Che Guevara, speak. He went home, and told his family they were leaving on an airplane that day, for Miami, and taking only what they could haul in suitcases. He knew what was coming. Many other Cubans played the denial game. They got many years to regret their decision to do denial. The lesson: get out of denial.

Non-traditional roles require more energy to maintain. Don't believe me, watch, and pay attention. If you can be around a happily married couple, watch carefully, as there is much learning there.

Two yang polarity people fighting is not heaven. I know, from personal experience, and the calibration of debriefing myself, that feminists will make my life hell. The only reason I can see, for feminists to marry, is to revenge themselves on all men, with one man. I've seen this pattern carried out often, including on me.

Given their agenda, they would be in a lesbian relationship, hating their artificially inseminated sons. Smarter men know that feminists and happy marriage go together like military and intelligence, or corporate and ethics, or honest and politics. I'm sure you could find one exception, somewhere in the U.S., but you'd really have to look.

I compete all day at work. Do I really want to come home, and compete? No, I want to get out of Yang, and into Yin. Even professional athletes take breaks, and sleep.

I was in a Sweat Lodge, once. We talked out our pain, among other things. One of the group was a self-described feminist. She said she had no idea men suffered pain. She didn't understand that men don't talk about their pain, normally, they just put up with it. Feminists literally do have models that unrealistic, of the world.

Katie Roiphe wrote a most fascinating book[100], where she noted that feminists had no problem with falsely accusing men of raping them. They also had no problem deciding, after the fact, that something consensual was actually rape. This was their way of fighting the patriarchy[101].

---

100 *The Morning After: Sex, Fear, and Feminism on Campus*, by Katie Roiphe. This is an Intelligence Summary par excellence, something every male college student should read.
101 I saw this in the Army. There was this one woman, who was, let's just say that if she walked down the hall, I had to turn and face the wall, to keep from reacting, or not being able to stand up straight. She came on to an E-6 promotable, a training NCO. He responded. She turned him in. He was court-martialed, busted to E-5 [dropped two ranks], and sent off to Korea. How do we know it happened this way? Because she said so. Every male who saw that took careful note of this most fascinatingly educational object lesson. They discharged her, later, for defrauding the government. The government didn't like getting screwed, and could actually do something about it. Yes, there is also sexual violence against women in the military.

If your name is Jesus, and you like paying, painfully, at length, for other people's sins, go ahead and date feminists. I knew a guy in college, who married a feminist lawyer[102]. She treated him with such gross disrespect, even the women in the office he worked in couldn't believe it.

He had a solution, though: beer. Lots of it, and often[103]. I know a better solution: stay out of it, to begin with. It has worked for drugs, for me, also. If you never get started, you never get addicted, or trapped. Default solutions, and least energy paths, work.

Every major addiction, and every horrible marriage, and relationship, started with that very first decision to enter into it. There were always intuitive warnings- feelings in the gut- that warned against it. My subconscious mind works to my benefit, and warns me. I can choose to listen, or not listen.

In my experience, it seems that feminists have this belief that they are somehow super-attractive to men, even when they are boiling over with hatred for them. It's the female equivalent of the pothead who thinks that somehow having old, dirty, smelly clothes, a 4 day beard, dirty, unkempt hair, and no job prospects somehow makes him irresistible to women.

Men over the age of 30, who have jobs, and some experience of life, are far more cautious. Most I've known simply find a polite reason to not pursue relationships with feminists[104].

---

102 Think carefully. This is someone who not only has a lot of residual hatred for your gender, she also knows many legal ways to hurt you. If she is at all capricious, or has bad moods, she can and will ruin your life.

103 I am not saying domestic violence (and rape), doesn't exist. They do. I've seen it myself. The majority of sexual violence is men on women. I don't do it. What's relevant to me is what can happen to me. Feminists refuse to acknowledge that yes, it can go the other way, too. I was married to a former police officer. She got drunk and angry enough that I was terrified she would cut my throat in my sleep. She knew how. I told my daughter to lock her bedroom door, at night, and I began sleeping in another bedroom. I got her out of the house as soon as I could. Norm Stamper's book *A Top Cop's Expose of the Dark Side of American Policing* even admits that female on male violence occurs. No, it's not common, but feminists denied for decades that it even existed. The fact that this exists is something to factor into any man's calculations. I know that woman trashed me about town, also- and whom would people believe? I left town. Why fight? She lies about other things. Liars are found out, eventually.

104 I was in a martial arts presentation, years ago. The speaker was fascinating. There were a number of women in the audience. After the class, one woman told me she had some good information about the instructor, but she would only tell me if I met her in a restaurant. It didn't

I have two daughters, a sister, and a wife. Do I want equal rights for women? You bet I do. I also want a happy life, and I have found that involvement with feminists is totally at odds, with that.

I remember a lass in my Calculus class, in college. She looked like she had stepped out of the pages of a women's fashion magazine. She was great, until she opened her mouth. She sounded like chalk shrieking on a chalkboard. Oh wait, they used something else in your school. OK. She sounded like an engine, racing, with a high whine, just before it blows up. She was full of resentment.

Eye candy is interesting. In nature, what kind of plants are the most colorful? Sometimes, the most poisonous. A woman who has been treated like the princess will expect to continue to get that high level of maintenance. She is high maintenance. Feminists are even higher maintenance.

Keep in mind that many cosmetics are toxic. The red shades of fingernail polish, for example, often have lead-based paint. Women swallow about half the lipstick they put on.

Anything you put on your body ends up in your bloodstream. Toxins are stored in the fat around the liver. I have no desire to be involved with a toxic waste dump. You'll never hear that in the media.

Consider carefully what the mothers of your friends, in high school, looked like? They were probably a little bit plainer, used fewer cosmetics, and most had a dazzling smile, from the heart, which they flashed. This is useful. They had results- families, with children. Copying from success can be useful.

Men over 30 may want eye candy, if they have the money, time, and energy for the high maintenance costs.

---

feel right. I asked my wife to accompany me, because I don't meet women alone, like this. It feels too much like walking into an L-shaped ambush site. She showed up late. She told me what she wanted to say about the instructor. She realized that yes, the large gold ring on my finger really did accompany a wife, and that my wife was with me. My wife mentioned she was pregnant, and the woman got up and left without saying anything. I am a nerd, and at times clueless. I asked my wife what happened. That woman, who was a militant feminist, was trying to hit on me. She realized she wasn't going to get anywhere, and left. Was this respectful? Is dealing with a woman who is totally disrespectful to me useful?

The smarter men think about more permanent qualities, like character, attitude, heart, dietary habits, energy level, propensity to bitch, and so on. They understand the energy gradient.

Some men- yes, some men- even write a LIST of what they seek, in a woman, so they have a clear image, and know what their priorities are. Cutting out 95% of the not useful field, in a search, with simple default rules, can be very useful.

I remember a friend, years ago, who dated a very, very bright woman. He told me she could run circles around him, for intelligence. However, they had problems. He went to counseling, with her.

Now think about that- had to go to counseling even <u>before</u> getting married. A sane man sees this a large blinking neon sign, from the Universe, saying *Here be Dragons*, and gets the heck out of Dodge[105].

He did so. He found a woman that he said was like a '50's housewife. They have a great time, being married, they go dancing, and really enjoy each other's company. He knew his priorities.

S. Two possibilities

Men evaluate women carefully, to see if she is "the one". Let's talk about two wives. Dr. Glenn Morris wrote fascinating books. He taught at a small college in Michigan. He was laid off, one day, and told his wife. When he got home from work, she had already laid out a plan. She didn't want to take the kids out of school, and she said he couldn't get another job locally.

So the plan was to get a divorce, she would keep the house and the kids. He would pay child support, and go off somewhere else. This plan was hatched in about two hours. He was, yes, a little broken up about it. He put it in a book he wrote, which many spiritually aware men have read.

---

105 For non-native speakers: this is a slangy way to say it was time to break off the relationship, immediately.

I know a woman, who grew up in New Orleans. She is in my mastermind group. Her husband called home one day to say he'd been laid off, from his ad agency job. She went out and bought champagne, cheese, and fruit. When he got home, she had a table set up, with that. She told him that they had to celebrate his going out on his own, to get out of the limitations of that job. He was somewhat in shock. She was supportive.

She mentioned some slight worries about this, in my mastermind group, later. I have paid attention to detail, pattern, and process, for a long time. I asked her if he was any good. She said he was always at the top of his class, and was great with the firm.

I said they were cutting their costs, to get rid of him, they figured a couple of newbies would be cheaper. I asked if he had taken any clients with him. He had. I said if he was any good, and delivered good product on time, that it would take about two years for him to wipe up the floor with [i.e. defeat] his old employer.

I said if his previous employer was stupid enough to be cost cutting, and getting rid of talented staff, they were also stupid enough to be putting their focus solely on getting paid, timely. I said they were delivering shoddy product, late, with excuses. I said the partners or owners were having $200 lunches, buying homes in Florida, probably a boat, and not putting time into the business.

I said this not even knowing the company. Two years later, she asked me how I knew. I said, "patterns". Her husband taught a class, in college, on what he did. It was packed. And he had more clients than he could service. Quality sells. BS is flushed away.

The first wife was rational, in her head. Yes, there are women who are this cold-blooded, and even more so. The second wife had heart. She understood patterns, and she was supportive.

If you were a man, which one would you trust your economic, and emotional health to? Which one is more likely to produce children that you could really enjoy, who would be successful in life? Which one would you commit to? Do you really think men over 30 don't have enough awareness to see this?

Patterns matter. I pay attention to patterns. They are like the swirls, in a lake, that tell you the fish, of subconscious programs, are moving, below the surface.

T. Default rules can work well

In any data processing search, you want to eliminate the elements that don't help you, as soon as possible. Default rules do this.

A friend of mine went wife-hunting. He needed simple, effective rules. He listened to his dates carefully. If they complained a lot, on a date, in fact if they were anything less than pleasant, that meant they were high maintenance. He crossed them off his list. A bitchy woman trying to be pleasant is kind of like Cinderella's stepsisters, in the Disney cartoon. They can't hide the bitchiness.

He also watched carefully how she treated people, particularly men, in service positions, such as waiters. Why? Because he knew that this was exactly how he would be treated, within six months. This is a measure of subconscious programming. I don't normally share "silver bullets" like this, but women who are disrespectful can't hide it. I'm not sharing all my silver bullets, of course. I paid too much, in pain, to acquire them.

His mother, who was very bright (and Jewish), tried to set him up with bright Jewish women[106]. He would have nothing to do with them. Intelligence is a fine thing, but not if it is used against you. He married a woman who might not be as smart as he was, and who had her emotions on her sleeve. He could tell if she was lying to him. He liked that[107].

---

106 My father told me to always cultivate people, to learn their gems. He said Jewish and black people were really important to cultivate, since they had been persecuted, which means the dumb ones got killed off, and only the smart ones survived. I have found that both Jewish and black people have a lot of wisdom, and will often share it with people who listen respectfully. This is also true of Native Americans, Orientals, and many other groups.

107 I lived in a cooperative dormitory in college. There was a very bright woman there, who had a boyfriend some distance away. She would take on a lover, about once a week, and dump the guy, to replace him, after a week. Her boyfriend didn't seem that smart, to me. I doubt she changed her habits after she got married. I wonder how he reacted, when he found out what he'd married. He may have found out after the kids came along, and the mortgage was in place.

A man with any brains at all knows that if his woman has no respect for him, he cannot trust her. He knows to get out as quickly as possible- with stealth, to get her to break it off, before the children come along.

U. Intent shapes the world: The List

This is a use of intent, a way to ask the Universe for what you want. I suggest doing this even if you don't want a permanent relationship now. This will give your life focus. You will know precisely what you want- what is useful, for you.

You will also avoid entanglements with what you don't want, which are not useful. My father once told me that the main reason for marriage is to raise children in a supportive environment, where, ideally, two biological parents take a strong, long term interest in the success of their kids. He said you can get whatever else you might want outside of marriage, but not that[108].

The focus of knowing exactly what you want is very useful. You will carefully weigh the value of casual relationships that you don't intend to last long. Be honest about your intentions. People respect honesty, and hate being lied to. I've found that people who reacted badly to respectful honesty are people I need out of my life.

Know your standards, for what you want. Then, don't settle for less, for the people you get serious with. Here's why. I remember a bus driver, who was living with a woman. He wasn't happy with her. She couldn't cook, she was cantankerous, always bitching and complaining, couldn't handle money, and very lazy[109].

He saw a woman, a passenger on the bus, that he really liked. But he couldn't act on it, because he was attached. He wasn't married. But he was tied down, as if he was. A woman that mean can easily allege domestic abuse, too, with no penalty if proven a liar.

---

108 Spain has been taking up the U.S. model of divorce settlements, that gut out men. As a result, unmarried men over 40, in Spain, keep girlfriends, but don't want to get married. Even men over 30 feel that way. Spaniards are pragmatic and grounded, and ask for help when they need it. Americans are pie in the sky idealists who already know all there is to know. Until Madame Pain makes her extended stay in their lives, that is.
109 Who is more foolish- the fool, or the fool who follows the fool?

It is better to be single and lonely, than married and lonely. Once you are involved, detaching isn't easy[110].

After my second divorce, I met a woman who was incredible. It was a fiery relationship. She was bright, beautiful, she had everything in the right place, sex was magnificent, it was liquid fire. She had everything I could have wanted in a partner. She had just one little problem. She could drink more booze than you can imagine.

Yes, she was an alcoholic. It was very painful to break it off, but after my second divorce, from an alcoholic, I knew I had to do it[111]. If you need motivation to break off from alcoholics, just go to an Alcoholics Anonymous meeting, and listen.

This intent method is called "The List", and smarter women also use it. After my second divorce, I was told about it, by a woman who got tired of what she was dating[112]. She completed her list, and "released it to the Universe", as she put it. Two weeks later he showed up, and they were married 3 months later. She was deliriously happy with him.

I did this, myself, after my second divorce. I had no intention of getting married again, I did it just to experience focused intent, and put the list away. She showed up, even so, with everything on my list.

It seems I matched what was on her list, also. I was at a seminar, where a woman said she did this, herself. He showed up. Her husband to be had only one item on his list: to find a beautiful woman who would love him forever.

I mentioned this to a cousin, who said, "Oh yes, I did that 25 years ago, and it worked." I was figuring, gee, I wish I had known that in high school.

---

110 After my first divorce, it literally felt like I had a limb ripped out, and I was bleeding, for a couple of months. That makes no sense to people who live a materialistic metaphor of life, but that's what it felt like.

111 My intuition started talking to me, saying, "*Yo, lights on, nobody home- what, you just divorced your second alcoholic wife, and now you want to go for number 3? You don't have enough pain in your life, is that it? And think about the children you'll have with this woman, before you are forced to divorce her, whose lives will be utter hell. Yes, this is definitely the woman for you.*"

112 See what happens, when you listen to people, with good ideas? You learn. This pattern is useful!

Had I done this, I would not have married either of my first two wives. I would have saved myself great expense, and a lot of pain. The electric fence is waiting. What lesson do you want to learn from it?

One of Ann Jirsch's books also talks about The List. It's simple. Make up a list of what you want in a partner. Then recognize that the one you seek is also making up a list. I have never seen the lists that men make in a book, and I read a lot[113]. They don't talk about it. OpSec[114] matters.

What if you do this (assuming you are female) and next week your soulmate hears you in the grocery store, bitching to your girlfriend about how you hate men, cursing all men? Guess what happens? You are permanently crossed off his list- and you never knew[115]. Here is some of the list I wrote up. This is important only as a sample. What is the guy/gal you seek writing about you[116]? Do you have qualities you can juice up, or improve, now?

1. Loves me completely [may need to be tested, under stress].
2. Healthy.
3. Has a heart, that is, cares about people[117].
4. Has a smile that flows from the heart, and really affects me[118].
5. Has worked in a real job, and knows how to handle money[119].
6. Balances me.
7. Relaxed, attentive, and not a drama queen[120].

---

113 A man wrote *The Art of War*, by Sun Tzu. May I recommend you read it, because smarter men over 30 think just this way. You will get a major education.

114 Operational Security- the need to keep silent about your plans.

115 Mahatma Ghandi said that life is a whole. You can't really do good in one area of your life, and ill in another. Life can only be compartmentalized this way, in fantasy. It is important to clean out the negative, as fast as you can, in all areas of life.

116 Now if you had some training, I could take you deep into trance, we could visit the guy's place, see what he wears, get the license plate off his vehicle, maybe his telephone number off the phone, find out what he likes, and so on. But that is way beyond the scope of this book. Jose Silva's outfit used to teach these skills. Here's the hard part, though; if you intend him any harm, even subliminally, his subconscious systems block your perception. Think about that.

117 Men know that heartless women are best avoided, unless they really want a lot of pain in their lives. Think *Snow White*'s stepmother.

118 Smarter men know that if she lacks this, they need to get the green stakes, garlic, holy water, and mallet out, whoops, I mean, to let the woman break it off ASAP.

119 This is real. My brother's wife put him over $40,000 in credit card debt. He was able to file bankruptcy before the laws changed, under Bush. She would buy expensive new things, and then garage sale them a month later, sort of like reverse investing.

120 A drama queen is a woman who wants to create her life as a Soap Opera, with all kinds of conflict, and challenges, who cannot leave well enough alone, who loves to argue and fight. I was married to two of them, and that was about five too many. There is no peace, with them.

8.   Admires her father[121], who also likes and respects me.

9.   Her mother likes and respects me[122].

10.   Likes children.

11.   Has the energy to keep up with everything she'll need to do, down the road, including waking up every two hours to feed and change an infant who also likes to cry a lot.

12.   Doesn't drink, smoke, or do drugs- she is clean, in other words.

13.   Cosmetics are full of toxic ingredients. If she uses a lot of them, this means her liver is stressed. Uses few to no cosmetics.

14.   Not addicted to shopping, which can be as bad as a cocaine addiction. Whatever else may be true, she won't change her habits. Either I accept her just as she is, or I get the heck out of Dodge, ASAP. Flowers may thrive in BS, but relationships don't.

15.   No tattoos, as they can cause skin cancer[123].

16.   Grew up in a loving family. Women tend to recreate what they grew up in.

17.   Took care of younger siblings, or other children.

18.   Watches positive media, and likes to read. If she watches soap operas, she will recreate what she sees, in her life.

19.   Her dog likes me. Animals can't lie.

20.   Patient.

21.   Likes sex, and nature.

22.   Speaks English, Spanish, and French, perhaps other languages also.

23.   Cultured, likes museums.

24.   Bright, perceptive, likes to discuss ideas.

25.   Enjoys and reacts well to positive attention: roses, cards, etc.

26.   Appreciates what she has.

27.   Enjoys seeing people getting helped, and enjoys helping people when possible.

28.   Small to medium breasts[124].

---

121 Women marry what's in their subconscious minds. If she hates her father, she will hate me, eventually.

122 My first wife's mother hated my guts, even before meeting me, and it went down from there. Women become their mothers. There is an Arabic proverb: Look for the woman [you want to be married to in 20 years], and marry her daughter. This is very real. My current mother in law refers to me as Saint Job, for putting up with her daughter. This is a good sign.

123 As they say in the Navy, it is better to not overspecialize, to be Mark 1, Mod 0, so you have more options. Tattoos limit options.

124 Watermelons are fine for summer snacks. Breast enhancement surgery results in significant problems, some years down the road, while 70 year old women with small breasts may still look great, as they do in France. Some guys do think ahead. Women with large breasts have probably

29. Nutritious diet, and good health.
30. Practical and pragmatic.
31. Intelligent, but without edge.
32. Shares my spiritual interests.
33. Never married before[125].
34. No children[126].
35. Self-reliant, strong, stands up for herself- and has no interest in feminism[127].

Barbara De Angelis has some quite fascinating books for women, on relationships. She has been married five times. I know, from experience, that mistakes and defeats teach much.

I read the one book she wrote for men, *What Women Want Men to Know*, more than once. It is useful. Of any books I've read for women, on relationships, hers seem the most grounded. Oh wait, you say, men don't read books on relationships, do they?   Uhh, yes, some do, especially those calibrating and learning after a divorce.

Then there is the Reverse List, the automatic reject list. Women have them, but don't seem to understand that men have them, also. Here is mine.
1. Takes drugs, alcohol, tobacco, or toxic cosmetics.
2. Low energy level

---

not developed the other parts of their character. Incentives affect behavior, and character.

125 Many, many older men put this on their lists. Maybe that might encourage you to choose your partner carefully, and not think of divorce as an easy out, huh?

126 I might consider marrying a woman with children from a previous relationship, however, I would evaluate it very, very carefully. The slightest intuitive warning, though, and it's over, forever. I know a woman who treated me with great contempt. She had just gotten divorced, and had three kids. She was going out with two men, hoping one would pan out as a husband. Neither did. So, later, she was particularly nice to me. I don't like two-faced people, and she was kind enough to share that intel with me early. I was quite happy to cut her off. May I say, also, she was gorgeous.

127 My wife has a friend, in Spain, who is fanatically feminist. She met a guy in a bar, once, and told him, "I'm tired of men who never call back. I want YOUR number, buddy." He gave her his number. When she called, he said, "just a minute", and blocked her out of his cell phone. She must have seemed to him to be on steroids. She starts talking that feminist stuff, and the men leave. She had a boyfriend. She constantly broke dates with him, because she felt badly, due to cigarettes and poor diet. He broke it off with her. She said good riddance, because he should have been attending to her every need. No. He knew a high maintenance woman, when he saw one, and cut his losses. She plays with minorities, and illegal immigrants. Feminists were doing the same, when I was in college. Men with brains gave them a wide berth- politely, and as invisibly as possible.

3. Bitchy, catty, plays emotional games[128]- for example, gets upset; when asked why, she says, "If you loved me, you'd know!" Gosh, I don't know, which means I don't love you. Thanks for the clarity! Be seeing ya. Gosh, I'm glad I found THAT out so quickly!
4. Has no heart, and is incapable of love.
5. Only her mouth smiles.
6. Has no idea how to handle money effectively.
7. Plays power games, or is a drama queen.
8. Hates her father, or mother.
9. Always getting sick, can't handle simple stress.
10. Promiscuous, or worse, mother is promiscuous.
11. Watches soap operas. Addicted to soap operas, Romance novels, and/or *Cosmopolitan*, or gossip magazines.
12. Hates animals and/or children.
13. Has feminist ideas[129].
14. Has no patience, and/or gets irritated easily, and often.
15. Doesn't like sex, or nature.
16. Constantly complaining.
17. Does little with her brain.
18. Materialistic.
19. Talks a lot about her horrible boyfriends.
20. Bitches all the time.
21. Children, if not extremely well-behaved.
22. Any other intuitive warning signs show up. No feedback, text, explanation, or proof is needed, if the gut level feelings show up, it's over.
23. Any other Threat Level Yellow, or Red, items.

I did a very thorough debrief, over years, of every relationship I ever had with a woman. I calibrate both the bad and the good. I know, intuitively, if a woman is lesbian, or has those tendencies, even if she doesn't. I can even use a Huna method, to tap into the feelings she has around specific subjects, such as men. I will never enter a relationship with a woman again, without extremely thorough intel up front.

---

128 This is the "Guess what you did to upset me, today" game. Video games are much better.
129 Danger, Will Robinson, Danger! Captain, five Klingon warships have decloaked, their phasers are powering up, and they are converging on our position. Recommend immediate evasive action. MAKE IT SO.

V. Being grounded is more effective

I had a French roommate, in college. He had a fiancee, in France. He had round glasses, and didn't look like a movie star, if you know what I mean. He had women hitting on him, all the time, he turned away more than he got, and he was never without. It was all physical, to him, he had no respect for them.

He could almost have set up one of those machines, like they have in the grocery store, for women to take a number. Remember, I lived with the guy, and could hear what was going on in his bedroom[130]. I saw it myself. He didn't boast. He was too busy getting it to waste time boasting.

We asked him what Francoise, his fiancee, would think. He said what she didn't know wouldn't hurt her, and besides, she must understand that he was a man, with needs.

Was that fair? No. But what does this pattern teach? Women fall in love with... their fantasies. There is a lesson here. Isn't that exactly the slacker problem? Falling in love with fantasy?

When I was in college, and the workplace, I noticed that many bright, attractive, seemingly nice women married jerks. It made no sense to me. Here I was, a nice guy... but women don't go out with nice guys, much, not when they are under 30.

They went out with bad boys[131], slackers, jerks, and con men. Women seem to be smarter in Europe, I've noticed, though.

I think I figured it out. They wanted to feel superior to their husbands. They wanted to change and mold them. I heard a joke about this: Men don't want their wives to change, women want their husbands to change a lot, and both get disappointed.

Then, when women are about 30 or so, perhaps with a kid or two, and it seems to hit them that they have made less useful choices. They recalibrate their standards for what they want in a man[132].

---

130 Since awareness is always beckoning, I did ask him what his silver bullets were, but I won't be putting them in print, ever. They were most fascinating. Who knows? I might need them one day. Though the Demographic shift just gets better and better, for me.
131 P. 120, *Calling in "The One"*, Katherine Woodward Thomas, New York: Three Rivers Press, 2004.
132 I knew a farmer, in his 60's, with an 8th grade education. He looked and dressed like a farmer. He was also very smart. He was dating women from the personals. He had a number of

It is almost funny to see single, professional women in their 40's, looking at adoption, or even artificial insemination, angry and resentful because professional men are largely unavailable to them, as husbands.

I don't think they understand how they scare away potential mates, with all that resentment. At an energy level, it is more powerful than skunkspray, and about as attractive.

Their male counterparts have better options, and not just due to the demographic shift. As I listen to Enya, on youtube.com, writing this, a popup ad came up, to connect men with Japanese women, or was it Taiwanese... what does it cost to put a popup ad on youtube, I wonder... how much money are they making, connecting men up with these women, that they can afford popups on youtube[133]?

There are around 40 companies that do nothing but connect American, and Western European men, with women in Asia, Eastern Europe, Russia, South and Central America, and even Africa. Think about that. One reason professional women can't find partners, in the Washington DC area, is that the men are outsourcing overseas.

My nephew was learning Russian, on his own time, a while ago. I saw his tutor. She was a Russian immigrant, long blonde hair, and very nice, none of the bitchiness you'd expect from an American woman. Omigod, if I was my nephew's age, and single, with a tutor like that, I'd have been learning Russian, intensively, on my own time, too.

My nephew worked in an office in Russia, for a short time. It was explained to him that he was expected to pick one of the women, there, to marry her, and do the whole Immigration thing to get her back to the U.S. Apparently every American man working in Russia can do this. The choices were splendid.

Russian, Oriental, Eastern European, South and Central American women, almost always have good hearts, like family, believe in marriage, and love children. They work hard. They have seen what mean, nasty men, and drunks, can do, and appreciate good treatment.

---

fantastically beautiful, well dressed, elegant dates. Why? Because of the demographic shift. That alone forces some recalibration.

133 Squaw is an insult to Native American women, and shouldn't be spoken. Here's why. In Aninishnabe, numsquaw means penis. 200 years ago, a Caucasian man could go to an Aninishnabe [Algonquian] village, tap his genitals, and say numsquaw, and it was understood he sought a wife. The more I study Native American culture, the more I realize how much wisdom they had. That was a predecessor to the war bride concept.

American men can be preferable to the local product, in many cases. There are no guarantees in life, of course, and they aren't all good.

Don't think that Russian, Japanese, or Chinese women are passive shrinking violets. Russian women have to deal with loutish drunks, raise the kids, work all day AND do all the housework. They are tough, really tough. Japanese and Chinese women? They work at a level American women mostly can't comprehend.

American women, in their 20's at least, tend to be high maintenance. They tend to not value men very highly, and seem to always want and demand more. They complain a lot. American women can change, as they get older, and life teaches them about realistic models of life.

The least energy path is the local product, however. And that is your advantage. If you choose to be grounded, then clean out the negative energy, and get into the polarity that is in harmony with your goals, you have the high ground, energetically. What is your energy gradient?

W. Don't see divorce as a convenient exit

Marriage, in the U.S., and even parts of Europe, is becoming a worse and worse deal, for men. I compare what my grandfather's generation had, to what my father's generation had, to what my generation has, and it is getting worse. The main single reason I see is that women don't commit to staying the course, aside from slacker mentality in men.

Never enter a committed relationship with the idea that you can just get a divorce, if it doesn't work out. This is very bad planning. Divorce does not end the relationship, it poisons it.

Are you a woman over 30? Unless you have a fantastic energy gradient, you are in the position of selling yourself as a used car, to a guy who knows cars. That metaphor is right on. Is he getting a good deal? For a man, getting married is kind of like playing a gambling game, where he is gambling his financial future on the roll of the dice. He can put his bets wherever he likes, but he will be affected by the choice, for the rest of his life, if he has children.

He knows he can lose big. Sit in at divorce court, if you doubt what I say. Watch what happens to the man. Then know that each one of those men carved up will affect another 10,000 men.

For a man, getting into a serious relationship is something like skydiving. Once he is out of the plane, he is committed. It feels dangerous, even with the best of parachutes, I mean women. Women love to find out they are pregnant, they start buying baby clothes, etc. Men get nervous, wondering how they will pay for it, because no matter what happens, they will be paying for it.

If you were skydiving, wouldn't you want to be sure the parachute was in good condition? That it was packed properly, and you had it properly strapped on your back, when you left the aircraft? Wouldn't you follow the sequence they taught you, about pulling the ripcord?

Did you really think men over 27, whose eyes have been opened by what happened to a buddy, aren't looking at women just as carefully?

The court actions around my first divorce cost about $1,000, when I was making $1,000 a month, in the Army, after taxes. It was uncontested. That is unbelievably cheap, most men I mention this to cannot believe it was so low.

My second divorce also cost me $1,000. She got a divorced female attorney, which is usually a recipe for a junkyard dog. However, I had no children with her, and no real estate, and was with her less than two years. This was also dirt cheap.

I have known simple working men who paid out a high five figures, or low six figures, just in divorce costs. Few people work to keep marriages together, but there is an entire industry of lawyers, guardians ad litem, government entities, and so on that profit from divorce. All of them see the man's economic assets the way slaughterhouses see cows, and most men over about 27 know this.

It is not unusual for divorce to completely wipe out a man's assets. The founder of Access Consciousness, Gary Douglas, was zeroed out this way three times, by divorces. I suspect he's a lot more careful now.

Women wonder why older men aren't very quick to commit. Are they that dense? This is why it is important to be aware, and to always be learning more and more, especially in areas where you don't know much. You get more accurate models of how the world works.

Do you remember Russian Roulette? Russian soldiers would get drunk, take a six shot revolver, with a round in one chamber, twirl it, and put the gun to their head, and pull the trigger.

There was a 1 in 6 chance of dying. Getting married to the wrong woman, for a man, is like playing Russian Roulette with 5 rounds in the six chambers. Don't believe me. Ask older divorced men. If they trust you, they'll happily tell their stories, in a motivating, visceral way that you'll never forget.

In Spain, until recently, for a man to claim paternity, he had to go to the *Registro Civil*, and sign papers. If he denied paternity, the child took the mother's last name, the father had no parental rights, and he could never be sued for child support. Julio Iglesias lives in the Dominican Republic, now. There are numerous Julio, Jr's, running around. And he isn't paying child support to any of them, because he never signed the Registro Civil forms to claim paternity. Blood and DNA tests aren't done.

The effect of this was that Spanish women were far more careful, and liked to be with a boyfriend for up to 10 years, so they could be sure they trusted him.

Spanish laws are being conformed to the American model, however. Divorces are more common, with divorced men sleeping in their cars because they can't afford both child support and an apartment, as in the U.S. Oh, you haven't seen that yet? Really? It's real to the men.

There's nothing quite like learning from other people's mistakes. Men do pay attention to this. Because <u>now men have to be the really careful ones</u>, with less legal protection than women have.

Marriage- *with the right person*- can be heaven on earth, though. There is a marvelous story by Hyemoyohsts Storm, called *Jumping Mouse*, which you can google. Jumping Mouse has a vision of the sacred mountain, and eventually gets there.

The honeymoon is the vision of what is possible. You have to go through the swamps of subconscious blockages to get there, however. Quitting when the first problem shows up doesn't get you there. It's like whitewater rafting- stay focused when you're running the rapids, and steer away from the rocks.

Sure, you can get out, and start another relationship. You discover that not only do you have the same subconscious blocks, but you have also been zeroed out, you have to start over, from the beginning, to work through them.

So. The smart thing to do is to start with someone who really likes you, who is cooperative, energetic, and supportive, and covers for you when you are down. This is why you do "The List", and reject what doesn't meet that standard. These are only words on the page, until you feel them in your body, as real.

If you are entering into a relationship while being very careful to note where the exit door is, this could be a signal from your subconscious mind to not enter it. Honor those signals. They are far less traumatic than pain.

Women can inflict pain on men. Many women do. They'll most likely get away with it- for a time. What goes around comes around, though. There may be no justice, but there is balance.

X. The major secrets to making relationships work

The first secret is, for a man, no finance, no romance. There are a very few creative artist, or slacker types, who can attract women for a short time. However, they are selling their skills to one customer, and this probably won't last. A man knows that if he wants a long-lasting romance, he will need the basis for assuring a regular income. That is very focusing.

For a woman, being pleasant, and supportive, and having basic skills, is very useful. That's not enough, any more, though. There is something even more fundamental. It is simple enough, but it's not easy. Most people are looking to be loved, to get attention, and energy, but they aren't willing to put out much, themselves.

The only way to get more than you give, is to give more than you get.

Choose your partner well. Then, always do more than your partner does. You never see all they do, anyway. Don't keep count, or cut things in half, just do more than they do, cheerfully. Do thoughtful things. Be respectful. Make your partner's heart sing, when you can. No, it's not easy, but it is very satisfying when you get a hit [succeed in this], and then a second one.

Men are actually very easy to please, as Dr. Laura Schlessinger points out. Feminists hate her guts, because she says that respecting husbands is helpful in marriage. She is saying things that were second nature to my mother's generation. I'm not saying I agree with everything she says, however, respect is powerful. Wisdom is wisdom, wherever it shows up.

Y. Energy Gradients

Why are women or men seeking a partner, in marriage? Isn't it because they'd have more energy, and happiness? The difference between what they would have, married to a great person, and staying single, is the energy gradient. If there is no energy gradient, they'd have no desire to get married.

A Native American elder was asked once how to grow quickly. He thought, and then said, "Always choose the harder road, when you can." I wouldn't say always, but this helps.

I am deeply spiritual. To me, questions are very important. Why do you want a partner? I mean, really?

The movie *The Bucket List* cites the ancient Egyptians as saying you get two questions, when you depart this life: *Did you find joy? Did you share it?* Dr. Raymond Moody, who writes on near death experiences, says the two questions are: *How much did you learn? How much did you love?* They really are the same question.

Why do you seek a partner? If filling their life with joy is not high on your list, you are a parasite. My nephew is of the slacker generation. He is very bright, and has a great job. Women are constantly trying to get their hooks into him. His defenses are finessed incredibly well. He knows exactly what he wants. He gets it[134]. He is making his choices. He hasn't found a woman he wants to let very far into his circle of trust, though.

---

134 He actually took Women's Studies courses, in college. He lets the feminists project their fantasies on him. He had one woman, umm, gosh she looked good. And when she wanted commitment, he went slacker on her. He is smarter than I am, in some things, I need to get that kid talking, soon, and take notes.

The Jabarian character, in the movie *Solaris*, says there are no answers, only choices. In this life, we get choices. When I am evaluating choices, I pay careful attention to how I feel in my body. I shut down resentment. If a choice feels really heavy, and constricting, I know to avoid it. If a choice feels light, spacious, and good, it's probably the right choice. Life is about making choices.

Choices involving relationships have major ramifications in life. I enjoyed Geometry, in High School. I don't use it much. There were no classes on how to get along with other people, though, especially with the other gender. How smart is that?

Were I running a high school, I would issue every student a copy of *How to Win Friends and Influence People,* by Dale Carnegie; *Men are from Mars, Women are from Venus,* by John Grey, as well as some of Barbara De Angelis' books. Life is about choices. Feel out your choices, weigh them carefully. There are consequences to all choices.

This chapter may be difficult for some to read. The White Man culture I live in seems to have forgotten how to do Truthspeaking. I am learning it. You can only change yourself. In changing yourself, you change the system you are a part of.

My mother remarried, at the age of 79, after my father died, to her college boyfriend. She has had some real happiness. Her new husband could have done many things, but he chose her. Could it be my mother's high energy level, smile, desire to speak only the positive, or just memories of college, in her energy gradient? I don't know.

I am happily married. We have a wonderful little girl. And so it is. Yet there is one more bit of awareness to share, for this chapter. I know a woman, who is extremely high energy, I mean, elfin energy. She is kind, unbelievably competent, smart, and any other positive adjective you can name. She has two kids. She is married, very loyal to her husband, and sterling in every respect. She gives more than she gets, in every situation she is in.

I am proud beyond measure to say that my older daughter is roughly in her class, if much younger. She has taught me much, by example. I first heard her speak when she was 23, two decades ago. Everyone in the audience was impressed.

She has chosen to do the best she could, to grow, to take the hard path, to always improve herself. I have dealt with crummy jobs. Hers is crummier than almost anything I've done. She does it extremely well.

She will never have to worry about the demographic shift, man/boy slackers, female/male ratio, Threat Level Red, or anything else we've discussed. She could have any available man she wanted, any time she wanted. She would need only to smile at that man, and that would be it. Her energy gradient is that high. I do not exaggerate. If anything, I have been very sparing in what I say.

Were she and I single, and I thought I had a chance, I would court her with enthusiasm, even if she were twenty years older than I am, no matter how many children she had. If it were ever to happen that she and I could get together, I would crawl over mountains, leap through fires, and throw heart and soul into making it happen. But she wouldn't pick me. She would have her choice of anyone she liked.

I aspire to be at her level of energy, competence, enthusiasm, rapport, and many other qualities. I give thanks to the Creator that put her in my field of view, so I could be humble, and know there is much more to learn, and more areas to grow in. I give thanks for the wisdom that empties my cup, so I can receive more awareness. She started out with no more than any woman reading this book has, right now.

She chose to follow the path of energy, the spiritual path, service, balanced with the material. She chose to be excellent. Service makes the saint. She has chosen that path.

What do you want to leave behind? I have chosen to be generous, to help those in need, to inspire people when I could, to take on difficult tasks. My life is the fuel for my mission and purpose. When it is time for me to check out, I want the fuel burnt up, in what is worthwhile.

The Peaceful Warrior said service to others is the highest calling. So it is. Everything needed to solve all the world's problems exists right here, now. All that is necessary is for people to reach deep into themselves, and serve each other. Follow your bliss, whatever it is.

Have you found joy?

Have you shared it?

How much have you learned?

How much have you loved?

How could you have fun, being of service, to others, today?

Chapter 7: Revenge of the Forsaken Gods

We have abandoned the rituals that mark the transition from being a dependent person, to being an independent one, from being one taken care of, to one taking care of others[135]. This is taught, not caught, as Dr. Sax notes at p. 166, by a community of men showing boys how to behave.

Dr. Sax cites the eight core values of a school, at p. 165. The Boy Scouts put it this way: A Scout is: Trustworthy, Loyal, Helpful, Friendly, Courteous, Kind, Obedient, Cheerful, Thrifty, Brave, Clean, and Reverent[136].

A. What do boys need?

Even the peaceful !Kung require that boys earn the right to be called men by a test of skill and endurance, as noted at p. 166, of Dr. Sax's book.

1. Ordeals

Dr. Sax, I loved your story about the Polar Bear Club, at p. 73. As you say, the boys got to shore, after being in the water, "feeling like a man".

Ordeals make a lot of the foo foo idiocy of our culture, including video games, just not very interesting. Indigenous cultures all had some sort of ceremony where they at least told boys, if not also girls, you are now a man/woman, we expect you to act like it. Only in this country do we not do that.

---

135 P. 132, *Calling in "The One"*, Katherine Woodward Thomas, New York: Three Rivers Press, 2004.

136 There is still controversy about their relationship to gays. My father remembered gays in the military, in the 1950's, and they were in during the 1980's, in my experience. Why is sexuality being forced on the Boy Scouts? How does that help? If the Boy Scouts openly let gays be leaders, this means about half their troops leave, and form their own organizations. Scout-like organizations were siphoning off members when the issue first came up. It also means that some single mothers start getting nervous about having their boys in the half of the troops that remain. Let's see how you like it: I am going to use the force of the law, to impose my own sense of morality on you, and cut your income by more than half, while I'm at it, so I can feel self-righteous. Let me give you the address to send your checks to. Do you like it? That is the choice that is forced on them. That's a lose-lose solution, but Americans love lose-lose solutions, and create them all the time. I am not opposed to gays, but people don't seem to understand that theory is not function.

So we get 50 and 60 year old little boys- like Presidents Clinton and Bush, who acted like little boys. These are allegedly leaders. We get little girls, too. Madeleine Allbright wanted to send the U.S. military into Yugoslavia, to do something they were never trained to do, under very bad conditions, because "well we have them, why not put them to use."

Psychological neoteny is not useful, among humans, and especially not among boys. Boys need ordeals, to mature. If they don't get legitimate ones, they get illegitimate ones.

In the mid 1990's, as I was waiting out my second divorce- from an alcoholic- I decided to do a VisionQuest. I spent 4 days in the woods. I put a stone out by the path, each day, so the groundskeeper knew I was ok. I spoke to no-one. I had no food, only water. There was no human contact, no media devices.

I did have a sleeping bag, and a poncho, and clothes. A hanblechia of the Lakota people wouldn't have had that, even. I was not able to stay awake all day and night. I was sick on the second day, and it got worse. On the fourth day, there was a breakthrough. I got the Vision. It was very subtle, and I didn't recognize it at first. It shifted me in many ways I cannot even model in language.

A culture stupid enough to deny boys a VisionQuest, or similar ordeals, to get out of the small, immature self, into the larger self of mission and purpose in life, is on the path to dying. Women did not traditionally do VisionQuests, in Native Culture, much, because they are seen as closer to source- they have to be, to have babies. Now that everything is out of whack, there are more women doing them.

If you don't know your mission and purpose in life- which always involves service to others- you are rudderless, in a stormy sea. How many thousand teenagers commit suicide, yearly? Of that number, how many knew their mission in life? 0?

Dr. Sax is precisely correct, when he says that maturity involves growing into service to others, awareness of one's larger self. Every Native American elder I ever spoke with hammered this point.

They don't respect B.S. as much as Anglos do. They seem a lot more grounded than most Anglos I know.

2. Paths to getting Respect, and other incentives

Native elders say that respect is the center of the circle of community. Why? Because from respect grows rapport, from rapport, trust, from trust, communication, and then cooperation. Cooperation is how humans survive.

My wife remembers that when military service was mandatory, in Spain, the parents always looked forward to when their son would come home, polite, <u>respectful</u>, and like a man.

Respect is very important. Respect motivates boys. If they can't see a path to getting respect, though, they take the path to disrespect, because at least that is attention, however negative. That is what Dr. Sax means by "raising status". This is one reason why boys avoid lowering their status- lowering their respect- as noted at p. 27.

How many awards are offered, in your community, for teenagers who do something really nice and positive for their community? Other than the Eagle Scout rank, that is. There aren't any, are there? What you put attention on grows, and energy flows where attention goes. Is this intelligent?

Idle hands are the devil's playthings, my grandmother used to say. And so they are. In the city I work in, an 11 year old boy was shot. They had helicopters, at $1,500/hour, they had police officers, who by way cost over $150,000/year, when you consider their logistical tail, they had EMT's, and all kinds of other specialists.

But the city is unwilling to fork out $20/kid/summer for programs to keep them occupied. Americans prefer to have memorials, pass feel good legislation, wring their hands, have marches, wear ribbons, and play denial games, in fact anything, except cheaply preventing the problem from happening in the first place. Ordeals can be very cheap, and safe. Americans can't stand cheap, safe, effective solutions, though.

This is in itself gross disrespect. The gross disrespect for men, particularly fathers- as Dr. Sax points out, notably with Homer Simpson- has an effect. Who wants to be an object of disrespect?

Let's imagine a kid in the ghetto. The responsible boy who grew up, married a woman, had children in wedlock, went to a crummy job every day, paid the bills, treated his woman with respect, avoided alcohol and drugs, and contributed to society- he's a chump. Or at least seen that way. The drug dealer with gold chains, the Cadillac, the ladies... gets respect. Is this an incentive for positive behavior? For service to society? In the burbs, the drug dealer becomes a financier, helping the current economic situation stay bad, for a profit. His kids buy their drugs from the drug dealers in the inner city. There is balance.

What is the incentive to do things worthy of respect, when those doing the hard work that society needs, get disrespect, instead? Nick Hockings, an elder of the Ojibwa nation at Lac du Flambeau, told me about an award, that the women of the tribe resurrected, from their history. It recognized men who had done sustained service to the community.

Oh wow. Native American women are remarkably smart, they understand incentives. A woman leading a spiritual class told me that Lynn Andrews writes fiction about indigenous peoples, which shows amazingly flagrant disrespect for indigenous men. I remember reading about some Native American women picketing one of her appearances, because they didn't like her insults to their men[137].

Can you imagine Anglo women, especially feminists, being upset about insults to Anglo men? I sure can't. They would heap on the insults, and find a way to propagate them more efficiently. Wow. Anything I can do for Native American women, I do. I went out to help an itinerant minister, working among Native American and Hispanic women, over a long time.

---

137 Alcoholism is a major problem among Native Americans, and Native American women have every right to be bitter. But they chose to look at the larger picture, instead. You know, every Native American I've ever talked to had fantastically valuable lessons in awareness for me, and very little tolerance for B.S. I have learned so much from them.

Respect is very powerful. Napoleon knew the power of medals. What is a medal, really? $5 of metal, and cloth.

Yet his troops would risk their lives repeatedly, for a *Legion D'Honneur* [LDH]. His spymaster would have preferred a LDH over the chests of gold coins Napoleon gave him. Why? For the RESPECT.

Where is the Legion D'Honneur, and twenty other medal types, for boys, for doing great things in their community? Dr. Sax's book points out that they get them for playing virtual games. Where are the rewards for service in the material world? What, there aren't any?

Who is really dysfunctionally lost in fantasy, the boys, or the idiot adults who didn't bother setting up effective incentives to guide the boys into positive activity that benefits society, and into maturity?

My father told me that being a father really meant something, when he was a boy. Are fathers men, respected, now? Heck no. Are mature, responsible men respected? No! What do you get for being a good father, and responsible husband? Ridiculed! The "responsible" father on the TV show *Two 1/2 Men* is ridiculed. The Charlie Sheen slacker character, who treats women as objects, is the hero[138]. Your eyes eat images the way your mouth eats food....

Let us consider the media worship of Hugh Hefner. This is a guy who has slept around on two wives, and several girlfriends. He is the living embodiment of immature slacker male sexuality. Yet even the women around him worship him. He wasted Barbi Benton's best years, but she still loves and respects him. I wouldn't believe it if I hadn't seen it.

Hefner's main aide, a woman, committed suicide, rather than roll over on him to a prosecutor. He is a multi-millionaire slacker. At one time he kept 24 bunk beds at his mansions, for playmates, and even now seems to have 4 girlfriends. My guess is that he has a 55 gallon drum full of Viagra pills, too.

---

138 See pictures of him without makeup, though. The Cocaine has taken its toll. Balance...

Brooke Medicine Eagle quoted a Native American woman, in one of her books, as saying that men become the kind of men women sleep with. Boys in high school notice who the eye candy is hanging out with. Football players... now there is a group that is an unmistakable example of responsibility, and service, isn't it? Football players are never arrested for assault, or other crimes, their spare time is always spent in service to society, isn't it? We want all our boys to be like them, don't we?

Did anyone ever think that the problems with *Boys Adrift*, in our society, no, most of our society's problems, are directly due to perverse incentives? Where is the respect going, in our society? It's not going to responsible men. Don't you think boys and slackers notice that?

Responsibility is not just ignored and disrespected, though. It's worse than that. I asked a guy who loved being a Boy Scout why he wasn't a Scoutmaster. He said he wasn't willing to gamble his future on the stability of an emotionally immature teenager who would never face consequences for making a false claim of molestation. Responsible men actually face a new Inquisition.

3. Limits

When my father was young, if a teenage boy mouthed off, an older male relative would pick him up by the lapels of his shirt, hold him against a wall, look him right in the eye, and say, in a quiet, very focused voice, "Don't do it again" or "Don't shame your mother again."

Yes, my father was also spanked with switches, which is not appropriate. But the talking to method worked. It was used even in the military, until recently.

These limits have all been removed. So, now, instead of solving the problem cheaply, when it is small, we prefer to pay the criminal justice system far more money, and to scar the boy for life, instead. This is beyond merely stupid.

4. Awareness of Mental models

Years ago, I heard a Schaghticoke [Aninishnabe] Native American woman tell a story. A boy came to her, to tell her that some other boys were killing frogs, for fun, and not planning to eat the meat.

In her culture, this is a major insult to the Earth, to the system, to the Creator. She went, and found the boys. "Oh", she said, "you are valiant warriors, finding food for the people. How are you going to cook those frogs, for people to eat?"

The boys looked up, shamefaced, as that hadn't been part of their plan. "You aren't planning to eat them? You mean you are just killing them, for fun? This is not the work of a warrior. This is waste. It is an insult. How can you expect the Earth to feed you, if you waste what it gives you?" The boys looked very ashamed.

What was her mental model? Boys as guardian warriors in training. Why would you have slackers as mental models? That makes no sense. No, she appealed to the model in them, of the guardian warrior, who helps the people- the larger self- and does not waste. She helped them along to becoming mature adults, with a mental picture that appealed to them.

Dr. Sax correctly notes that we don't have mainstream cultural stories of real boys becoming real men. We have *Braveheart*, and *Gladiator*, and *Star Wars, Harry Potter*, and *Lord of the Rings*, but no boys becoming men in our era.

And then we wonder why boys prefer fantasy to boring reality? To quote Mark Twain, are people really that stupid, or are they just having us on? Oh wait, there are movies about boys becoming men in our era, Guardian Warriors, even. *Spiderman*. Oh wait, that is also fantasy.

Dr. Sax notes that gender matters. This is like saying that drinking water matters. It is one of those truths that is so mundane, it is almost invisible. But he actually has to say this, because people don't seem to be aware of it.

Dr. Sax cites *My Three Sons* as an example of a wise father. Hmm. I heard a radically conservative religious person say that shows like *The Odd Couple, My Three Sons*, and *Family Affair*, which all involved two men as a couple, was part of the gay agenda to get homosexuality approved by society. Well, I left that milieu. I would have picked *The Rifleman*, or *Daniel Boone*. But ok. Dr. Sax is right on to say that modern media attack responsible men.

Dr. Sax, what you eat with your eyes, you become. TV shows do shape our culture. The most influential Nazi anti-Jewish movie was not *The Eternal Jew,* as most textbooks will say. That movie was a box office bomb, even though Adolf Hitler personally oversaw its creation. Josef Goebbels, Minister of Propaganda, had rules for effective propaganda. It had to reinforce existing prejudices, slightly and subliminally, and it had to be entertaining[139].

The most effective Nazi anti-Jewish propaganda movie was *Jud Suess*. Don't watch it. I watched just 20 minutes of it, in translation, 60 years after it was made, in the context of a different time, language, and culture. I found hatred for Jews welling up from my subconscious, shortly afterwards, something neither I nor my family ever cultivated. It took me a week of serious effort to clean that out. How powerful was two hours of that movie, in the German culture it was made for, in 1943? Dr. Sax, do not doubt the power of images.

[140]All of us have some kind of mental map, that we file information to, which we use to help us navigate in the world. However, the map is not the territory. One example of a mental model is the "Life is Hard" filter, or transparent belief. This filter affects all of experience in life. It is not necessarily true; I've known many people for whom life was easy, and even a celebration.

"There are no good men out there" is also a transparent belief. It makes its holder blind to the good men out there. Slackers operate out of mental models, also. Faulty models of how things work mess up life.

---

139   I wrote propaganda in the military, where we used those same principles. Propaganda is written to these emotions: Fear, Hate, Hope, and Curiosity. The newspapers in my area actually sort their articles in this order. The front page starts the fear, and hate.

140   http://www.joshuakennon.com/mental-model discusses this, some. Joseph Campbell's Monomyth, which is the basis of all mythic stories, and successful movies, is also interesting.

There is no such thing as defeat, or failure. There is only quitting before reaching success. There are no mistakes, there is only learning. The only quality successful people share is persistence. These models work.

5. Staying in the question, not leaping to conclusion

The human egg, once it accepts a sperm, changes so it won't accept any more sperm. The mind can be like that, once it accepts an idea. Nietzsche said that the new truths are never accepted. The old folks die off, and the young, who have grown up with the new truths, accept them. Max Planck said something similar. The limiting belief is "That's just the way it is", or "that's the way we've always done it."

If we want change, we have to abandon our sacred cows, and be open to change. The subconscious mind is a cybernetic mechanism. If you put a question to it, it will seek the answer until it either finds it, or is told to stop. A conclusion stops this process.

Your life is the crystallization of the questions you ask. If you are asking the question, "Why aren't there any good (wo)men out there?" you are asking the powerful part of your consciousness to tell you why. It will give you 1,000 good reasons. It will keep doing so, until you CHANGE YOUR QUESTION. When you start asking the question, "How do I find the good (wo)man out there, for me?" You get totally different answers, because you changed your question.

Dr. Sax asks a very important question: what does it mean to be a man? He offers one answer: service to others. Right on, dude! And another question: Who wants to be Homer Simpson? Right on, dude!

Then he asks, what about girls? This question is easily answered. Read any woman's magazine. Women torture themselves for hours, comparing themselves to photoshopped perfection. Photoshopped perfection... wait a minute, we saw that before.... oh yes, porn is photoshopped...

I don't see any difference between porn, and the pictures in women's magazines. I guess each gender likes looking at them, but neither is particularly healthy, don't you think? If nothing else, don't both kinds of porn foster unrealistic expectations, that are bound to lead to frustration?

How could we focus our attention more productively, so we get what we want?

6. Mentors

Somehow, aside from school, teenaged boys need mentors, who guide them. I don't know what form this would take. I would say that every healthy society I've ever looked at had mentors.

Dr. Sax understands this. Role models who are worthy of respect is a great idea. Respecting those same role models is also a good idea. Restoring the bonds between generations is a great idea. I was particularly impressed by the need to have real stories. People live their stories, in their lives. The story of Joshua L. Chamberlain is a good example.

John Nicolas put it so succinctly. What boys need is a sense of purpose, of who they are, so they don't have to play the game, and wear the mask. Teenagers want to do fun stuff, as is noted at p. 220. We need communities that provide appropriate paths for that.

Dr. Sax cites the toxic beliefs that substance abuse is normal, sex is sport, and violence and death are entertainment. These exist because healthy channels weren't open. I think these may also exist due to diet, and we'll discuss that later. We need more healthy channels.

How can we create those healthy channels, now? And have fun doing so?

Chapter 8: Detox

A. Changes needed

The most important questions to ask are during the debrief. In the military, the debrief is the most important part of the mission, because that is where the learning takes place. You figure out what worked, what didn't work, asked how you could improve. You might ask systems questions, like if this problem exists, what similar problems exist? What solutions are already being used?

Dr. Sax mentions a need for changes in education. I agree with that. Waldkindergarten is the way Native Americans taught their children, as noted in the book *Blossoming the Child.*

Legal outlets, and focused enforcement, is a good way to deal with street racing. Following up with a real challenge is a great idea. Reducing medication use is a great idea. Dealing with endocrine disruptors is a great idea.

Dr. Sax proposes some useful new belief systems:

1. Real men love to read.
2. What really counts is who you are, not what you look like.
3. Real world achievement matters (and can be fun!).

I would add a few more, in the form of questions, as in the book *How to Improve your Community: Over 30 ways to improve your community, quickly, and in the long term, even if you are working by yourself, don't have a lot of resources, never had training, and have no idea where to start* (used with permission)

-If our community were perfect, what would it be like?
-What's missing from the way it is now?
-How can we work together, and have fun creating a bit of that right now?
-What's stopping us? How can we have fun working around that?
-How can all players have more fun, healing our communities, through our work?
-What other people can we cooperate with, to do the job better, and to

do things no one agent could do alone?

-How can we make it "Win-Win"?

-How can we serve more people in a better way that is more fun? More effortlessly?

-What are people's interests?

-How could we have fun locating resources to feed those interests?

-How can we give people more hope?

-How can we work with local leaders better?

-How can we grow leaders of leaders?

-In looking at goals, how would we describe them for an elf who had no concept of adjectives? How could we make them so specific a child could understand them? How could we make an exciting picture of our goals, perhaps as a collage or treasure map?

-What available resources could we put to better use? How?

-How can we celebrate small victories better?

-How can we reward positive behavior better?

-How can we turn apparent enemies into allies?

-Who doesn't fit into our community? How can we reweave them into it, so they can have fun expressing their unique gifts?

-How could we speak to the ideal person inside everyone we meet, so they would sometimes act in an ideal way?

-How can we so fascinate people with community healing efforts, how can we help them have so much fun, that they forget about TV, violence, and the other time wasters they engage in, and have fun pitching in and creating a healthy community, together?

-How can we find great fascination in learning to use our attention, and respect, to bring a new, healthy community into being?

-How can we work together to fascinate and inspire people, with better stories, respectful attention, and other tools, so that they laugh, play, and enjoy life, and abandon all the negative things they do, because they just weren't interesting any more?

-How could our programs be so powerful, so fascinating, so enticing, that even violent and immature people recognized that it was just a lot more fun to mature, and work with others cooperatively?

-How could we create a local economic system so compelling, so fascinating, so inspiring, that everyone pitches in to make it sustainable, and we employ everyone in useful work?

-How could we create that same economic system, in the next 5 years, so that everyone has a job, some residents acquire assets, and everyone is incorporated into a healthy community where their needs are met, and interests fed, with the opportunity to pursue happiness and their mission in life?

-It is a known maxim in community development that more than enough resources exist to solve all problems. How can we reconnect community systems so that every nightmare people live now becomes a forgotten memory, preserved only in dusty archives?

-Since beauty is food for the soul, how can we add more beauty in our community?

-How could we help everybody realize their heart-felt dreams, effortlessly, joyfully, and lovingly, as we realize our own?

B. Your life is the crystallization of the questions you ask

Life is like wandering through a vast, dark warehouse of possibilities. Asking questions is like turning your flashlight on, and noticing a map to get you where you want to be.

When you put a question to your subconscious mind, it will seek out the answer, until it finds it, or until you tell it to stop. That is important. I know you've seen people asking questions about how they can do as little as possible in life, and still get by. Their lives aren't very interesting.

If you want to change your life, start by asking new questions. Tony Robbins has a two page section on what he calls power questions, in *Awaken the Giant Within*. I have been fascinated with these for a long time. The book *Quantum Power Questions* lists more power questions. Everyone I knew, who did well in college, had some very interesting core questions.

Asking questions like "Why are boys adrift? Why are boys maturing only physically?" does bring up answers. A better question would be "How do we engage those boys in life, so they enthusiastically choose to mature?". These get better answers.

I used to love the Chuck Jones question, used to create the Warner Brothers' cartoons, including Bugs Bunny. They asked what people would least expect.

The team that creates *The Simpsons* asks the same question.

What is your dream, in life? If you had no limitations, at all, and you could be anything you wanted, what would you be? That is very important. Now, for a more important question:

What would it feel like, if your dream was real, right now?
What would you see, hear, and feel, if you already had whatever you seek?

Wouldn't it be fun to spend time in that state of being, now, even if only a little? 90% of success is having a clear intent[141]. Then you could take action as you feel guided to do so.

C. Illusions: Killing the messenger

There is a story that the ancient Persian kings would kill the messenger who brought bad news. This means nobody wants to bring the bad news. *The Godfather* had a rule for his staff: tell him the bad news immediately. That is a systems approach. Feedback is always important. The Emperor's New Clothes is a story about killing the messenger, feedback, and denial. Our culture is full of these.

The beginning of healing is acceptance- seeing things just as they are. This book tells truth, as I've experienced it. You can deny it, you can kill the messenger, as you please.

D. There are only two choices in life

There are basically two choices in life: fear, and love. I regret many of the choices I made out of fear. I don't regret any of the choices I made out of love.

These translate, in action, into cruelty, or violence, and kindness.

---

141 When I made the decision to create this book, somehow the entire Universe started helping me. It was as if books on my shelf jumped out at me, with pages opened to useful ideas. The idea of helping others energized this, also. Goethe's statement on this, cited in Dr. Sax's book, is relevant.

If you knew that your every act towards others would be passed on to over 1 billion people, would you choose violence, or kindness?

Most people are not very spiritually advanced. They will copy you, and will pass it on, like the concentric rings that result when you throw a pebble in a pond. Every person you meet is a collection of fantastic lessons in awareness, which they will often share, if you treat them with respect. To quote many Native American elders,

Respect is the center of the circle of community

From respect grows rapport, from rapport, trust, from trust, communication, and from that, cooperation. Cooperation is how humans survive. Native elders note that competition makes people stupid, and point to political speeches, and Congress, for those who need rock solid proof. Respect doesn't mean you have to like them. When I learned that most people are doing the best they can with what they have, I lost a lot of harsh judgments.

A football game, isn't that competition? Or is it? What kind of cooperation was necessary to train the players, to build the stadium, to get the players to the stadium, to process the audience into the stadium, to sell the T-shirts, and food? Even that icon of competition is 98% cooperation.

How can we start cooperating, to solve society's problems? How can we restructure the incentives, to solve society's problems?

We must *be the change we wish to see in the world.*

- Ghandi

At its more powerful level, the above means we have to become, to enter into, to broadcast at the frequency of, what we wish to see in the world. We have to model it. Mark Twain said that you might be the only Bible some people ever see; what are they reading in your behavior? We could expand that, to say that you might be the only spiritual master some people ever see; what lessons are they learning, from watching you?

E. Something else Dr. Sax may not have considered

Our bodies cannot handle all the toxins we get, from the environment. We can see Autism Spectrum Disorder, ADHD, OCD, as canaries in the coal mine, metaphorically. Detoxification is necessary for everyone, nowadays, to be healthy[142]. Environmental exposures, including vaccines, can alter metabolic pathways and immune system responses[143]. Some Guatemalans refuse vaccines, because they say that vaccines make their children mentally retarded. In 1983, there were 10 shots on the vaccination schedule. Autism was 1 in 10,000. Now 36 vaccines are given, and autism is close to 1 in 100[144].

We have seen a huge increase in autism, asthma, allergies, and ADHD, in the last thirty years[145]. In one comparison, vaccinated boys were 155% more likely to have a neurological disorder, 224% more likely to have ADHD, and 61% more likely to have autism[146]. ¾ of flu shots available still have mercury, as thimerosal, as a preservative[147]. Vaccines may have formaldehyde, MSG, and a number of other toxins[148].

If your body can't keep up with all the toxins, they start building up, in the body. The resulting condition might look like arthritis, Alzheimer's, ADHD, autism, or others[149]. The behavior reported for Boys Adrift is not only typical of people with acidic body pH, it is also not unusual for persons with high toxic loads in their bodies.

---

142 P. 129, *Healing and Preventing Autism: A Complete Guide,* Jenny McCarthy and Jerry Kartzinel, M.D. New York: Dutton, 2009.

143 P. 250, *Healing and Preventing Autism: A Complete Guide,* Jenny McCarthy and Jerry Kartzinel, M.D. New York: Dutton, 2009.

144 P. 283, *Healing and Preventing Autism: A Complete Guide,* Jenny McCarthy and Jerry Kartzinel, M.D. New York: Dutton, 2009.

145 P. 247, *Healing and Preventing Autism: A Complete Guide,* Jenny McCarthy and Jerry Kartzinel, M.D. New York: Dutton, 2009.

146 P. 289-90, *Healing and Preventing Autism: A Complete Guide,* Jenny McCarthy and Jerry Kartzinel, M.D. New York: Dutton, 2009.

147 P. 297, *Healing and Preventing Autism: A Complete Guide,* Jenny McCarthy and Jerry Kartzinel, M.D. New York: Dutton, 2009.

148 http://www.cdc/gov/vaccines/vac-gen/additives.htm (updated April, 2008)

149 P. 144, *Healing and Preventing Autism: A Complete Guide,* Jenny McCarthy and Jerry Kartzinel, M.D. New York: Dutton, 2009.

Removing the poisons, changing the diet to keep food toxins low, getting rid of heavy metals in the body, and improving the diet, may cause these symptoms to dissipate or disappear completely[150].

Ritalin, and similar substances, are given to 20% of the nation's children. Diet is a contributor to ADHD[151]. Soda with high fructose corn syrup, alone, changes my behavior drastically. If I ate the kind of diet Boys Adrift ate, my behavior would be worse than theirs. I know this from direct experience. My older daughter got no vaccines at all. She is healthy. My younger daughter was given vaccines; she got fevers of 108 degrees F., each time she got one. Her body was giving feedback. Perhaps that also has something to do with her diagnosis of autism, now.

I remember a doctor lecturing on one reason for the wave of hippies in the late 1960's. A vaccine was contaminated with a simian retrovirus. Those who got the vaccine got the simian retrovirus, which changed their behavior. They didn't like bathing, didn't have much ambition... oh, gosh, they sound a lot like Boys Adrift. I'm sure that wasn't the only thing that brought hippies into existence.

Toxic bodies in nature generally can't conceive babies. It is possible to force conception, with strong hormones, however, the children pick up toxins from the mother's body.

I am not a doctor, and so would not be able to offer medical advice. I can say that overloading bodies with poisons is probably not going to result in optimum performance. Overuse of video games is described in Dr. Sax's book as having an autistic effect. Could it be that the toxic overload in the bodies of Boys Adrift is having an autistic effect, which makes video games addictive? I don't know.

I have done Dr. Richard Schulze's 30 day detox before. I get nothing for saying this, however I feel great, really good, after completing one. I believe there are other such programs on the market, as well, which could well be very effective.

---

150 P. 145, *Healing and Preventing Autism: A Complete Guide,* Jenny McCarthy and Jerry Kartzinel, M.D. New York: Dutton, 2009.

151 Pp. 246, 250, *Healing and Preventing Autism: A Complete Guide,* Jenny McCarthy and Jerry Kartzinel, M.D. New York: Dutton, 2009.

One thing is sure: if we don't address this problem, soon, we will simply die off, for lack of ability to reproduce. Lead from lead pipes, in Roman cities, added lead salts to Roman drinking water. Where is the Roman empire now? Long gone. There seems to be a cycle, in history: a new, energetic people come in, they civilize, their diet degrades, gets more acidic, and toxins build up. In time, that civilization collapses.

We have high tech to speed up that process. Do we have the sense to stop it?

F. Exploring diet

Health, and an alkaline body chemistry, that is, a body with an average pH of between 7.1 and 7.365, energy, and ambition, go together.

In Ayurvedic medicine, coffee, chocolate, and tea are considered Rajasic, or passionate, however they are believed to cause some damage, and to unbalance the body, emotions, and mind. This includes hot foods, and food with strongly bitter, salty, or sour flavors. The Rajasic diet of Ayurveda is basically a high protein diet, for laborers and warriors. The Sattvic diet is basically vegan.

Tamasic, or "darkness" diet is interesting. Tamasic diet includes large quantities of meat[152], especially if not fresh, especially from animals that are confined, with no exercise to get the toxins out of their systems, and covered in manure, as most animals in feedlots are.

---

152 Why meat? When you eat a lot of meat, your stomach has to become extremely acidic, to digest it. If you eat a lot of meat, regularly, the body has to stay more acidic. A pound of beef can last a Chinese family for a week, because they use meat as a flavoring, not as a main course, normally. Chinese Taoists traditionally avoided most meat, except for fresh venison. Native Americans could be very healthy, eating meat, but keep in mind the animals it came from were eating a very healthy diet, with no drugs, no hormones, and no feedlots. They got lots of exercise, which meant bowel movements that emptied them of toxins, quickly. Meat, for the more settled tribal nations, was also only rarely a primary part of the diet. Gathered plant foods were usually about 80% of their diet. Linda Runyon has noted that the kind of plants Native Americans ate were far more nutritious than anything you can buy in the grocery store. ¼ cup per day, of those wild foods, is enough, because it has such high nutrition. Any more, and you feel like you've had a Thanksgiving dinner. These foods include dandelions, lamb's quarters, amaranth, and so on. They are disturbed earth plants; you need only to dig a little, in the earth, and they grow as weeds, without further cultivation. The earth still sprouts healthy vegetation.

It includes most bread[153], cakes, curds, fermented foods[154] including alcohol, fish, mushrooms, pastries, and so on. Food that is deep fried, frozen, overripe, preserved in cans or bags, processed, rotten, spoiled, stale, tasteless, too sweet, and underripe, are generally Tamasic, and acidifying. So are tobacco and drugs.

Animal meat nowadays is full of drugs, including enough penicillin to cause penicillin allergies in people. Baking powder, candy, cooked pepper, excessive salt, mustard, pancakes and anything made with processed white flour[155], soft drinks, sugary jellies, irregular and binge eating, eating late at night, foods too cold or too hot, and foods cooked in aluminum tend to be acidifying[156]. Chronic dehydration, as noted in the books of Dr. Batmanghelidj, tends to acidify the body. Over 80% of Americans are chronically dehydrated, and don't know it.

---

153 Seeming wheat allergies could be to the insecticides and additives in the wheat, not the wheat itself. Sprouted seeds tend to be alkalinizing. My parents used to make it, it was good. It is also called Essene bread. What they did was to run the sprouted wheat through a meat grinder, form it into a loaf, and bake at a very low temperature. The Essenes would let loaves bake in the Sun, just like harvester ants do. Some people mix in raisins. It is a heavy, dense loaf.

154 Humans have eaten foods raw for all of their existence on the planet. Cooking is a more recent thing, and is necessary for some foods. Fermenting is more recent, and human body chemistry hasn't had as much time to adjust.

155 Grains of two thousand years ago were totally different. There were three kinds of wheat, Einkorn, Emmer, and *Triticum aestivum*. There were also non-hybridized barley, millet, and rye. These grains had more protein content than today's grains. Todays grains were hybridized to resist disease and pests, which means they have more glutens, lectins, and phytates, which can cause allergies. Let's remember that today's crops are sprayed with pesticides and chemicals, and grown in low nutrient soil. The USDA wrote an urgent report on the demineralization of soils, and the bad effect on crops. In 1936. Some who are allergic to modern wheat don't react to Einkorn wheat in small amounts. Traditional cultures know to get the toxins out of their food. For example, Native Americans knew to soak acorns from red oak.
Traditionally, grains were fermented, soaked, or even sprouted, as part of preparation. This could happen due to how they were stored, also. Sprouts are extremely nutritious, and toxins are greatly reduced. These grains were "whole grains", with all the nutrition present. Chewed sprouts are digested slowly. Flour was cold and coarse ground, with stone, and fresh. Ultrafine modern flour, with most nutrition removed, is digested quickly, and becomes sugar. There were no pretzels, or pastries, or hydrogenated vegetable oils, or canola or cottonseed oil full of pesticides, or high fructose corn syrup, or additives, or commercial yeasts. Grains were developed by populations in arid areas, as a way to expand the food supply. In the ancient Near East, state level societies are marked by the granary, and temple, inside a fort. Grain is associated with scarcity, and governments that deal with that scarcity, all over the world. The Aztec empire was dependent on maize. Grains could be stored, like military MRE's, but that didn't make them as nutritious as other foods. Grains were hard times food. The "sweetmeats" referred to in *1,001 Nights* was what is now called halvah, made often with sesame seeds, which is far healthier than candy. Sesame seeds have more usable calcium than dairy products, for example.

156 In *Childhood Diseases*, Dr. John Christopher, citing *Back to Eden*, by Jethro Kloss.

Ayurvedic practitioners say a mainly Tamasic diet harms both mind and body, by draining life energy. It takes more energy than it gives. Tamasic diet is a net negative for nutrition. It leads to strong urges to cause harm, along with a lack of ability to reason things out.

Tamasic diet further interferes with the immune system, and alters the neural pathways in the brain, causing mental disease, and unhealthy habits, including overeating. Overeating is related to food which has little nutrition. The body doesn't get the nutrition it needs, so it's still hungry. This was called the "munchies" when I was in college.

The ancient Hindu scholars knew that the Tamasic diet dissolved ambition, morality, spirituality, and physical health. It made people insanely selfish, and unexplainably sick. It caused people to do random and senseless violent actions. It fostered psychopathic behavior, horribly violent behavior like what we could call steroid or road rage, due to amygdalic hijack, and so on.

Have you watched the TV News, lately? It is the detailed track record of a Tamasic culture. See what criminals eat- liquor, and junk food, both of which are very acidifying. Red tinted fingernail polish, especially from China, often uses lead-based paint. Many cosmetics have heavy metals in their formulae. Anything you put on your body is absorbed into the bloodstream.

Aluminum, from aluminum pots, and anti-perspirants, even anti-caking agents in flour, has the frequency of sadness. Women swallow about half of their lipstick, which is made from petroleum. It's like drinking motor oil.

The modern American diet is more Tamasic than anything the ancient Hindus could have imagined. The top three killers of Americans, which kill more than 1 million Americans each year, are heart attacks, stroke, and cancer. All three are, at least partially, diseases of the fork[157]. Americans are digging their early graves with their teeth[158].

---

157 Kevin Trudeau put out a couple of books on what they don't want you to know. Whatever you think of his methods, his books are right on target. *Eating on the Wild Side: The Missing Link to Optimum Health*, by Jo Robinson, discusses how modern food has had its nutrition removed.
158 If you think of drugs as food, the 80%+ of all firearms deaths due to the drug trade would be in this number, as well.

All three are the direct result of a spiritual practice of consuming lots of Tamasic food, dead food, that comes in its own convenient plastic or metal coffin.

G. Some solutions

Dr. Sax correctly implies that there is no one thing we can do, to solve the Boys Adrift issue. The issue is too complicated for that. In software programming, they say "Garbage in, Garbage out", or GIGO. The "garbage out" of Boys Adrift was discussed, and some of the "garbage in".

In WW II, the concept of "Time on Target" was created. Let us imagine that an occupied European town, or fort, was full of German troops. A set time- say, 0933 hrs, on a particular day, was picked. All artillery, direct and indirect, from mortars to howitzers to 155mm long guns, and 240mm if available, was timed, so that all rounds would hit the target at 0933.

The effect of everything, together, was much more than the mere sum of the parts. It was devastating.

Metaphorically, solving the problem of Boys Adrift, and the larger societal problems for which these boys function like mine canaries, will require a similar combination, on the "garbage in" side of the equation. The combination will include every element in Dr. Sax's book, and others, also.

I have to wonder if our culture is willing. Our culture still practices human sacrifice[159]. Drugs and toxic substances are never properly tested, before use. When my first daughter was born, only 12 drugs were known to have no overt teratogenic effects. Other drugs had never been tested for damage to fetuses. Over 200,000 new toxic substances enter the environment every year. The list goes on and on.

---

159 Consider the waste of human capital, in prisons. Consider war. Consider those who die in their prime, of heart attacks, due to preventable causes.

Perhaps you are willing, for the small area you control? That's all we need. Slavery was banned in the British empire, because four people got together, and started a movement. I believe we can start a similar movement, to ban slavery to our abysmally poor diet, toxin overload in the environment, and all the other factors that create Boys Adrift.

I know we can, because I was a Boy Adrift, myself. I had to solve the problem, on my own, with very inadequate information. Following you will find a few ideas that I have found useful.

Fasting is nature's surgery, it cleans out the waste products. Animals that are sick will often fast, out of instinct. A basic rule of health is to eat slowly, chew food well, and avoiding overloading[160]. If that's too much, you can do a juice fast, with freshly made organic fruit and vegetable juices[161], and doctor's advice if necessary.

You are what you eat. So cows fed processed manure, and dead animals, make what kind of food? Is it any wonder that so many people, especially politicians, and media people, are full of s...? That condition starts, literally, by being full of s..., from crummy diet, and slow bowel elimination, which keeps toxins in the intestines longer, so they go into the bloodstream, instead of down the "drain".

Lemon juice, especially fresh, tends to be alkalinizing. Raw honey is alkalinizing. So, lemonade made from these was actually a health drink, at one time. The traditional Vermont cure for alcoholism is, first, a tablespoon of old-fashioned apple cider vinegar, like the Bragg stuff[162].

---

160 My wife's father is a retired officer in the Spanish Army. I asked him if Spanish soldiers in Basic Training had 5 minutes to eat, as I did. He said something very revealing. He said that Spaniards cannot imagine being limited to 5 minutes to eat, under any conditions. Latin countries, especially Spain, have a food culture. Food tastes good, and people enjoy it, slowly. Spanish restaurants do not rush customers out, to increase their "turn", as do some restaurants in the U.S.

161 If you need a model, I like Dr. Richard Schulze's *Common Sense Health and Healing*, and *There Are no Incurable Diseases*, which can be downloaded free at his website, herbdoc.com. Paul Bragg's book on fasting is useful. 1 800 HERBDOC used to send out the CD *Get Well*, for free, with a catalog of their stuff. My wife listens to that just for the motivation, it is more motivating than most positive thinking CD's. I get nothing for saying this.

162 Not the grocery store rotgut, I mean the Bragg stuff, or something similar, which you may need to go to a health food store for. I know it's an acid, but somehow it alkalinizes the body. Sugar is basic, but somehow it acidifies a body. *Folk Medicine,* by D.C. Jarvis, and *Back to Eden*, by Jethro Kloss, discuss this.

This is mixed with a tablespoon of raw- note that, raw[163] honey is required- in a glass of water, drunk every hour, until the addiction passes[164], which it does as the body enters the healthy alkaline pH range of 7.1 to 7.365.

George Ohsawa pointed out 40 years ago that disease germs cannot live in a body with a healthy, alkaline pH. Dr. D.C. Jarvis points out that a body with healthy pH sucks the liquid out of germs, and they die.

I have found that I eat and spend less, and feel very, very much better, if I eat a healthy diet. I saw the movie *Supersize Me*. I read the book *Fast Food Nation*. I listened to Dr. Schulze's CD *Get Well,* and looked at www.neadusa.org . At some point, I committed to eating a healthy diet, if only because my daughters need a live father, not one buried because he ate dead food that wasn't really food.

I may live in a Koyaanisqatsi[165] world, but that doesn't mean I have to be a part of it. Don't believe me. Try just two weeks, on an alkalinizing diet, and see how you feel. When I shop, I look at the price per pound. Dry lentils are about $1/lb, where I live. Added water cuts the price considerably.

Boxed cereals cost $6/lb, last I checked, and they are basically wheat flavored candy, with "fairy dust" vitamins, that is, approximately a teaspoon dropped into 5,000 gallon vats of cereal.

My breakfast now is a blender drink of fresh raw apples, alfalfa or soy sprouts, with a bit of ginger, and a few other things. I read that apples are more stimulating than coffee, and I've found that true. I take Cayenne pepper with garlic, in water, and that wakes me up more than coffee, Red Bull, Coke or tea[166], just as Dr. Schulze says it does.

---

163 This means raw. It does not mean pasteurized, or filtered. Raw honey is about the consistency of wax. If it is liquid, it is probably not raw.

164 Dr. D.C. Jarvis discusses this, in his books.

165 This is a Hopi word, meaning a world that is horribly out of balance. Native Americans see it, also, and are very worried about their own Boys Adrift.

166 People invariably ask what about travelling? Dr. Richard Schulze notes that Burger King offers veggieburgers, at least in parts of the U.S. Raul Molina, the host of *El Gordo y la Flaca*, on Univision, who loves food, and eats in restaurants all over the world, points out that of American fast food restaurants, only Subway uses somewhat fresh ingredients, with a minimum of additives, preservatives, flavor agents, and so on. I find that small family restaurants, which are Vietnamese, Mexican, or Indian, in my area, usually serve fresh food, overseas, also. *Fast Food Nation* points

When I can get Biodynamically-grown vegetables and fruits, I get them. They are beyond merely delicious. I eat wild plants, and feel great when I do. I try to live a balanced life, with enough exercise, rest, fun, and service to others. Dr. Richard Schulze's 20 basic rules, as noted in his book *Common Sense Health and Healing*, are a good foundation. Paul Bragg's and Kevin Trudeau's books have been helpful.

My grandfather grew up eating organic food. There were no pesticides. His family cow had milk with 8% butterfat. It was not homogenized, and it was healthy stuff. We can't go back to those days, however, we can improve our diets greatly.

A woman I know asked me about juicers. I said to just get one, and test it. She did so. She thanked me for that advice. She notes that she feels better and better, drinking freshly made juices, and is cutting back on the junk food. We may have to make the necessary changes one on one, and if that's the case, let's get started. Our children will imitate us.

In what ways could you begin detoxifying your physical body, and environment?

How could you begin detoxifying your subconscious mind, of belief systems and attitudes that are no longer useful to you?

How could you use questions, to focus your attention on activities that are useful, and bring you what you want?

---

out that food processors use flavoring agents to make food taste and smell really good, so you don't know how good food is by the taste, or smell. There is a popular chain restaurant, in my part of the country. Their food tastes really good. I got to thinking how they prepared it, how long it had to have been in the freezer, etc., and I realized there was no way their food could taste that good, naturally. I quit eating there. Something didn't feel right.

Chapter 9: Purpose in life

I heard the Wampanoag elder Manitonquat say that the purpose of life is to gather in all the awareness, and so on that you can, and then to pass it out freely, to all who will receive.

Boys Adrift... as if a boat was adrift... as if it didn't have direction, or a rudder, to guide the boat. What is that direction?

The purpose of our lives is service[167]. Anything less is an insult to the spirit. If you don't have a lot of meaning in your life, could I suggest that you commit random kindnesses, just for fun? In today's society, going against the cruelty promoted in all forms of media, to be kind to people, makes you a guardian warrior, by itself.

I knew a Boy Adrift. I have no idea how he got into college, his writing was atrocious. But he was in. He was also open to guidance. So I cheered him on. When he was ready to quit, I told him winners never quit. I told him successful people share the same quality: persistence. I gave him used books to feed his interests. I made a point of only seeing the ideal person in him, and ignored anything that was not that[168]. I do this for many other people, I didn't think this was that much.

He invited me to speak at the church celebration of his graduation from college. I was one of a handful of people who spoke. He said I did far more for him than his own father did. Now that is sad, I didn't do that much. I still help him; he needed help filling out a resume, and his parents had no idea how to help him. This was beyond their experience. Perhaps part of his issue was that his father was married to another woman, when he was conceived.

---

167 *Ask not what your country can do for you; ask what you can do for your country.* -John F. Kennedy

168 What you concentrate on grows; energy flows where attention goes. Do you remember those people, when you were young, who could only see your faults, your bad points? Didn't you just want to get as far away from them as you could? Then there were the people who could only see your good points? Didn't you just want to bask in that energy? Do you see the power, and incentive, of respect? I've seen Native American elders doing prison programs, who used respect to turn hardened criminals around. Manitonquat, who has run prison programs for 30 years, has said that he felt he could reach the heart of the worst criminal, if he had the time. You won't see the interesting work of Native American elders in prisons, though. The media has another agenda. Manitonquat is a guardian warrior in every sense of the word. He battles ignorance, and resentment, and hatred, metaphorically just like the Prince in Snow White cutting through the thorns, and the dragon of hatred, to finally reach the heart. Manitonquat, or Medicine Story, has books out on healing communities, which I found fascinating. He is a Korean War veteran, who does what he does out of pocket. I have no idea how.

He made some serious mistakes, in life. He had no guidance, he sort of stopped going to school. He graduated high school in prison, due to selling drugs.

He had some trouble finding even part-time jobs, due to this on his record. Some jobs are permanently closed out to him, due to his record. He has two children, with a woman he is not married to.

What was it worth, to help him? It felt great. I don't suppose I'll see any money from it, but then again, there is always balance.... Service is fun, and deeply satisfying. It gives life great meaning.

Here is a powerful discipline: your children don't listen to you- they imitate you. They follow your example, for good or bad. If you screw up, royally, they will, also.

As Native American elders, including Manitonquat, tell me, we are all here to help each other out. This book is a way to pay forward the help I've gotten. I'd like to live in the following question, for a time:

How can we have fun cooperating, now, to solve the problem of Boys Adrift, and then the larger problems of society?

Whatever else I've said, that question is the heart of this book. This book crystallized from that question. It could have been better, it needed more of this and that. As with all artistic creations, I have had to abandon it, to "freeze the design", as they say in engineering, and could never perfect it. Systems Theory, Quantum Mechanics, Chaos Theory, and so on are chipping away at the Newtonian/Cartesian world that put us in our current mess. I am very hopeful for the future.

Chapter 10: Boys Adrift are canaries in the mine

I've learned a lot from Native Americans, notably the books and trainings of Manitonquat/Medicine Story, of the Assonet band of the Wampanoag Nation, Nick Hockings, of the Lac du Flambeau branch of the Ojibwa nation, Dovie Thomasson, Kiowa/Apache, and Stalking Wolf, of the Lipan band of the Apache Nation, among others. I express my great appreciation for the patience of focus of all of the Sensei that have taught me. I would not be alive, now, were it not for their help and guidance.

Roy Bohm was one of the founders of U.S. Navy SEALS. SEALS are far beyond regular military personnel. They are trained to do ten times as much, they are leaders of leaders. Roy went looking to find the people he needed, and found many in military jails... adrift.

As we look at Boys Adrift, and consider the complete toxic load they carry, both at the physical level, in their bodies, and at the psychological level, in their subconscious minds, we can consider that it is a wonder that they are even alive. That they are alive is a testament to the adaptability of the human body and spirit.

If we choose to help them clean out their toxic loads, we can and will find among them the leaders that will solve our intractable problems. Doing this is not just a good idea, it may be necessary for our survival.

We have more problems in our communities than just boys. Boys Adrift are canaries in the mine. As we address those issues, perhaps we could begin to consciously recreate our communities, to meet everyone's needs. Possibly something like the following could guide community leaders everywhere[169]?

---

169 The following is from *How to Improve your Community: Over 30 ways to improve your community, quickly, and in the long term, even if you are working by yourself, don't have a lot of resources, never had training, and have no idea where to start.* Used with permission.

OUR MISSION:

Creating a healthy, entrepreneurial teaching/learning community that takes care of and solves most of its own problems while they are still small, that naturally resists addictions, where persons and organizations can and do focus on reaching long term positive goals instead of "putting out fires", where people take care of each other, like they used to, where everyone can and does pursue hisher mission and interests in life, developing "leaders of leaders", with "win-win" mutual support.

BASIC PRINCIPLES

The following principles are the guides for healing and developing individuals and community relationships at their five levels: mental, emotional/ social, vocational, physical, and spiritual. Speaking as one community, which seeks to heal itself, we seek a new way of living, from a new awareness, that will heal our problems, and allow us to sustain and enhance our community. We recognize that our problems are growth opportunities.

HEALING Beginning within ourselves, and working together in common interest and well-being, we endeavor to heal the conditions that cause social, psychological, and physical illness, addictions, drug abuse, and crime in our families. Among these are:

-a solely punitive approach to crime, and misbehavior
-abysmally poor diet
-media that promote toxic belief systems, including that substance abuse is normal and fashionable, sex is sport, and violence and death are entertainment
-the loss of appreciation for the strengths and gifts of our neighbors
-the neglect of hope, faith, and opportunity

We will work together to generate an atmosphere of appreciation, commitment, conviction, cooperation, creativity, expectation, joy in service to others, joy, respect, and the following:

A PLACE AND TASK FOR EVERYONE A community has a place for everyone, or it is only a faction. All people must be actively involved, using their unique talents. We work to involve everyone. Every person will be treated with respect and dignity, regardless of income, social involvement, age, prior actions, or other characteristics.

Everyone will be accorded the opportunity to contribute to the community, to heal, to participate in collective and personal growth, and to share the benefits of this growth.

ABUNDANCE   We already have everything we need for restoration and growth. The resources in our community, those of human potential and those of capital assets, are many. What we lack is simply the acceptance of these strengths, the confidence in our intentions, and the "bridging" of resources to interest. Seeing our abundance is to be one blink away from seeing complete fulfillment of our goals.

ACCUMULATING MERIT, aka "GIVE-AWAY"   We intentionally give out to others everything we can offer, without expectation of return from the recipient. Instead of collecting the contributions of others for our own use, we approach relationships with the sole intention of contributing all we can to the greater community. Healthy community begins within the individual, extending to each relationship, family, community, and nation. Lasting growth cannot be made independently of any of these entities, nor can it overlook the impact it will have on others. The seed is planted within ourselves, and cultivated to extend to all those around us. What we do for ourselves becomes what we give to others. What we give to others we will be giving to ourselves. Life is a circle, a system, we cannot give anything away without getting a return, somewhere.

ALL ACTION IS VISION DRIVEN   Vision is the seed around which all positive efforts crystallize. Where there is no vision, nothing positive occurs. What we concentrate on grows. We form an exciting, motivating, clear, detailed picture of what our community can be, when it uses all of its strengths, values, and contributors.

BALANCE   We consider the ramifications of our actions, and work to balance our lives. The center of life is spiritual. Spirituality and meaning in life are the same thing. Heart-centered approaches tell us what to do, and the "head" tells us how to do it.

COMMUNICATION IS HEALTHY   A community is a web of relationships which is more than the sum of its parts. A relationship IS communication. Anything that improves communication improves the community. Friction is how diamonds are polished, and it is essential to community growth.

COOPERATION   Cooperation is how humans survive.   Even a football game, an icon of competition, is 98% cooperation: to build the stadium, to get fans in their seats, to train the teams, &c. We will find new ways to cooperate.

CULTIVATE COMPASSION, PATIENCE, JOY   Where there is understanding, there is no conflict. In compassion, we accept the pace at which change occurs, and with patience celebrate each small triumph, every step taken, no matter how modest. Joy in all efforts creates ever increasing fulfillment. Our work is a cause for celebration!

CULTURE   Our city is rich with cultural pride, wisdom, and diversity. We encourage expressions of ethnicity, and strive to learn more about the cultures of our neighbors. We respect differences, seek common ground, and come together in an atmosphere of mutual learning and celebration. We recognize diversity as a highly positive characteristic, found in every creative city of the past, from Rome to Timbuktu to Muslim Spain to many others.

DEVELOPMENT IS FROM THE INSIDE OUT   All individual and community healing flows from within to the outside. Developing local "capacity" and sustainable activity is absolutely essential to effective use of outside resources. People must be actively engaged in the process of their own growth and development.   Without participation, there is no development.

EMPHASIZE THE POSITIVE   Since what we concentrate on grows, we emphasize the positive at every opportunity, building on what we have.

GROWTH AND GOALS   Humans and communities are goal-oriented, and are happiest when they are working towards positive goals. The creator put fun on the earth to mark out correct solutions.

KNOWLEDGE GAINED MUST BE SHARED TO BE COMPLETE   There is no wisdom without willingness to give. The experiences we gain in any of our programs and activities will be shared with all who seek them from us. We further reach out to others whenever possible, to assist them with the knowledge we have gained.

RESPECT Respect is the center of the circle of community. It is the right of every person. Since what we concentrate on grows, we respect and honor all positive activity and achievements in our community, and each person in it.

SYSTEMS There is a path of balance at the center of each individual and community, which can be found and followed. The community is more than the sum of its parts. Accurate moral and ethical boundaries serve the community and individual. Addictions are a direct result of imbalanced communities and lives. Each person has a Mission in life, and they are happiest when they are following that mission. All problems have the seeds to their solution within them. We seek solutions that solve many problems at once, synergistically, in a "win-win" fashion that benefits all. Because every living thing is connected to all living things, and because we are all linked in the family of human kind, any aspect of our growth, healing, and development must be interconnected to that of all others (personally, socially, culturally, economically, politically, etc...). When we work on any part, the whole is effected.

TOOLS: STORYTELLING[170] Traditional cultures communicated positive community values through storytelling.

TOOLS: FOLK DANCE[171] Traditional communities also used this. Healthy indigenous communities expressed "community" through the medium of folk dance, involving a circle. Folk dance is a traditional method of working off kinaesthetic energy.

UNITY We need the contributions, acceptance, encouragement, and support- the "mirror" of others, to develop and grow. Unity is the starting point for renewal, and as renewal unfolds, unity deepens. We use "win-win" approaches wherever possible. We vent privately, with friends, before meetings, never during, and concentrate on the positive.

---

170 National Storytelling Association POB 309 Jonesboro, TN 37659-0309 www.nsa.org

171 You might try "Encyclopedia of Associations", in your library, or google, for folk dance groups, or perhaps use an Internet search engine. One outfit that has picked up a number of indigenous folk dance forms is the following: Dances of Universal Peace, North America PO Box 1401 Blythe, CA 92226-1401 www.dancesofuniversalpeace.org

WE BECOME THE CHANGE WE WANT TO SEE   We become living models of the truths we want in our lives, for all to see.

WORK WITH WHAT WE HAVE   We use what we have, first, effectively. Diversity is a sign of health in nature and in communities. We seek sustainable processes and activities.

OBJECTIVES

CHILDREN AND YOUTH   We seek to create a drug and addiction-free, vibrant, healthy community where:

.Abuse is consigned to the history books

.Adult issues are addressed without trauma to children

.Children are challenged to the extent necessary to foster healthy growth, learning essential life skills like discipline, trust, respect, and problem solving

.Children feel supported, grounded, with opportunity and hope in a positive future

.Children grow healthily, and are allowed to be children

.Children have positive growth opportunities, and responsibilities

.Children have positive guidance and secure environments

.Children learn tools to address pain and anger, their range of emotions are respected, and they have ways to express emotions healthily
.Children's physical, emotional, spiritual, and vocational needs are addressed, in addition to their mental needs, and they enjoy balanced health in all areas

.Family and community traditions, such as ritual and bonding processes, and rites of passage are practiced

.Healthy relationships with elders and others occur

.Inter-generational ties are strong, parenting skills are commonly practiced, and role models are in evidence

.Parents are very involved with their children

.Peer mentors work well

.People learn from children and youth

.People recognize the effect of their actions on children, and choose positive activities

.Shortcomings are accepted, and people work openly to overcome them, without stigma

.The community welcomes its responsibility for raising children

.The responsibility of raising children is joyfully returned to parents, grandparents and community, rather than leaving it by default to formal institutions and the media

.Youth are respected and respectful

.Children are honored, esteemed, and respected as human beings, by themselves and others

PEOPLE We seek to create a drug and addiction-free, vibrant, healthy community where people:

.are respected and esteemed by others and themselves

.are so involved in positive activities that feed their interests they have no time or energy for negative pursuits or addictions

Boys Adrift: a response to a seminal book 138 ©2013 all rights reserved

.are spiritually healthy, free from addiction and a need to abuse, empowered with a healthy sense of self-esteem, respected and loved as members of their families and .communities and positive role models for children.

.have community support, encouragement and acceptance for their growth, transformation and self improvement

.have opportunities to grow and express themselves in relationships, family, community life and all other spheres of life.

.have opportunity, security, education, autonomy, employment, opportunities for expression, and support

.have supportive, healthy, loving relationships

.have their basic needs met, from within the community wherever possible, using outside resources in an integrated way

.know who they are, and have so many positive opportunities have opportunities to contribute to family and community

ELDERS   We seek to create a drug and addiction-free, vibrant, healthy community where:

.Elders express a mental, physical, emotional/social, spiritual, and even vocational wholeness which inspires all members of the community

.Elders live in health, in support, free from dysfunctional patterns, providing guidance to youth, and sharing the journey of healing and growth with the younger generation.

FAMILIES   We seek to create a drug and addiction-free, vibrant, healthy community where:

.Families are secure, save havens, in mental, emotional/social, vocational, physical and spiritual balance

.Families have internal and external mutual support, that reinforce positive activities

.Families operate at an optimum level, where each member's needs are met, free of addiction and abuse, supportive of the continued growth and development of everyone in the community

.Useful community values, such as kindness, respect, love, honesty, generosity, unity, responsibility, caring, empathy, sharing, discipline, commitment, nurturing and humility are modelled and practiced

ECONOMY, EDUCATION, AND GOVERNANCE We seek to create a healthy, vibrant, drug and addiction-free community, where:

.A healthy, sustainable economy promotes financial self-reliance, systemic health, and moral and ethical accountability

.Cooperative coalitions of leaders with vision, and clearly defined short and long term goals, produce a healthy economic condition in the community

.Everyone has useful, meaningful work

.Government assistance is used to create self-sufficient people and employment

.Leaders are constantly developed

.Leaders are role models

.People become contributing citizens, living up to the American ideal

.Resources to create opportunities for all are constantly gathered and used efficiently

What other items would you add to this list?

9405310R00080

Made in the USA
San Bernardino, CA
16 March 2014